THE AGES OF GOD BOOK II

# THE
# NEW HOLY SPIRIT
# AGE

**MICHAEL SHENTON**

The New Holy Spirit Age by Michael Shenton

This book is written to provide information and motivation to readers. Its purpose is not to render any type of psychological, legal, or professional advice of any kind. The content is the sole opinion and expression of the author, and not necessarily that of the publisher.

Copyright © 2023 by Michael Shenton

All rights reserved. No part of this book may be reproduced, transmitted, or distributed in any form by any means, including, but not limited to, recording, photocopying, or taking screenshots of parts of the book, without prior written permission from the author or the publisher. Brief quotations for noncommercial purposes, such as book reviews, permitted by Fair Use of the U.S. Copyright Law, are allowed without written permissions, as long as such quotations do not cause damage to the book's commercial value.

ISBN: 978-1-951670-53-5 (Paperback)
ISBN: 978-1-951670-54-2 (Digital)

Printed in the United States of America.

# CONTENTS

**INTRODUCTION** .................................................................................................. V

**CHAPTER 1** The New Holy Spirit Age ............................................................. 1

**CHAPTER 2** The Fullness of the Victory that Jesus Christ won on the Cross ................................................................. 11

**CHAPTER 3** Your Right to be a Child of God ................................................ 17

**CHAPTER 4** Impartation and the Laying on of Hands ................................ 35

**CHAPTER 5** Levels of Anointing ................................................................... 43

**CHAPTER 6** The Work of the Holy Spirit ..................................................... 71

**CHAPTER 7** I call you friends—God's Favour ............................................. 87

**CHAPTER 8** The Body of Christ ................................................................... 105

**CHAPTER 9** The Future of the Church ....................................................... 119

**CHAPTER 10** The Circumcision Party ........................................................... 125

**CHAPTER 11** The Works of God - through me and others ......................... 133

**CHAPTER 12** My Journey ............................................................................... 155

**CHAPTER 13** Baptism .................................................................................... 167

**CHAPTER 14** Revival Starts in Australind, 1999 (Bunbury Revival) ...... 171

**CHAPTER 15** The New Apostolic Age ...... 181

**CONCLUSION** ...... 205

**ABOUT THE AUTHOR** ...... 207

# INTRODUCTION

THANK YOU FOR PURCHASING this book, *"The New Holy Spirit Age."*

This is part of a series called the *"Ages of God."*

I am humbled that you purchased this book, and I pray that it blesses you with knowledge and wisdom through the leading of the Holy Spirit.

I pray God will bless you in all areas of your life in Christ Jesus, including wealth, success, prosperity, good health, peace, tranquility, and wisdom.

In 2003, I wrote a book called *"The New Apostolic Age."*

This new book, *"The New Holy Spirit Age,"* completed in 2022, builds on the knowledge and wisdom discussed in the New Apostolic Age.

The *"New Apostolic Age"* was a book that can be used as a manual to increase your relationship and Love for Jesus and increase your spiritual gifts. It includes teachings on working with the Holy Spirit to advance the Kingdom of God. Most importantly, we need to understand that the Holy Spirit is a Person. The Holy Spirit is the Person that was sent to be our Teacher, Our Guide, and Our Counselor.

The *"New Holy Spirit Age"* is a book that will teach and help you how to operate at a much higher level than discussed in the *"New Apostolic Age."*

Obviously, since 2003 I have grown spiritually in the Holy Spirit and Jesus, and I now have way more to share some 16 years later.

Later in this book, I will explain how we are now entering a *New Age of the Holy Spirit*.

My main focus in writing this book is to equip you, other Christians, and the Church, to operate in much greater *faith* and *power* much like the first Church operated when the Holy Spirit came upon them at Pentecost and afterward in the Book of Acts. However, as I spent time with God, I became stronger, and the Anointing of God became stronger. Now, the time has come for the fullness of Revival to be manifested on earth. God is manifesting this Revival thru many people and organizations. All Jesus needs is for people to obey the Holy Spirit. This is how all revivals have started—*OBEDIENCE is the key.*

Very recently, Jesus told me to restore *"The fullness of the Victory of Jesus Christ."* This is The 'Full Victory' that Jesus won for us when he was crucified and rose from the dead.

The opposition to the 'Fullness of the Victory' of Jesus began very early in the Church's history, even at the Apostles' time. Peter received great opposition when he went to speak to the Gentiles.

I see other men of God speaking out on these teachings as well. As the spirit moves in people's hearts and the churches, these teachings will become more prominent.

If you believe that Jesus is the Son of God you have the right to certain 'Promises.'

Jesus gave many specific 'Promises' that people who believed in Him would receive.

1. Forgiveness of Your Sins

2. Salvation and Eternal Life—you will never Die.

3. Your Right to be a Child of God

4. The Gifts of the Holy Spirit—you will receive power when the Holy Spirit comes upon you.

5. Impartation and the Laying of Hands to receive the Holy Spirit and the Gifts of the Holy Spirit

Today, we generally receive the *Power of the Holy Spirit* through Impartation which is *Praying and the Laying of Hands* to be filled with the Holy Spirit and the Gifts it bestows. When I teach these subjects and then pray for people, I see them having life-changing experiences—being transformed to bring forth such an amazing abundance of fruit to advance the Kingdom of God. I should say that I am in the middle of a war with the Kingdom of Satan. Every Christian is in this war with Satan, whether they understand it or not. Therefore, it would be wise to arm yourself with the potent weapons Jesus provided.

God told the Nation of Israel when He led them out of Egypt that He was giving them the land, a land flowing with Milk and Honey; even though they had God's promise, they still had many wars and battles to fight before they possessed the land.

We have the fullness of the victory that Jesus won on the cross, but we will still have many wars and battles to see those promises come to pass in their fullness and take the land.

This is further complicated by God's times and seasons when these victories occur.

One of the most important weapons is *Unconditional Love*, which Satan has no defense against (Unconditional Love).

*Unconditional Love* keeps no record of wrongs; it was *"Unconditional Love"* that defeated Satan when on the cross, Jesus said, *"Father forgive them for they know not what they do."*

Any Christian who hates his brother or anyone else has already lost the battle and works for Satan. I see some Christians harbouring hatred (if not close to it) in their hearts for other Christians, Churches, denominations, groups, etc.

People try to draw me into these arguments; my answer is always the same, *"God has not appointed me as a judge. How can I possibly understand God's actions with all the different parts of his body?"*

The *Test* for whether someone is in Christ is not their theology, but can they say that Jesus is their Lord and Saviour? This is the only *Test* to discern who belongs to Jesus; there is no other

*Test*. I repeat—the only *Test* is whether they can say Jesus is their Lord and Saviour. No man can say Jesus is Lord except by the Holy Spirit.

There are only two great Powers or Kingdoms operating on this earth:

**The Kingdom of God**
**The Kingdom of Satan**

By your fruits, you will know which Kingdom is operating in you.

**God:** *Love, Joy, Peace, Patience, Kindness, Goodness Self Control, Submission to Jesus, Faith, and Gratitude*

**Satan:** *Hatred, Murder, Division, Accuser, Anger, Bitterness, Resentment, Unforgiveness, Fear, Complaining*. With Satan, nothing is ever good enough. You cannot trust God. You are chained by Depression and a sense of Hopelessness.

You can belong to Jesus but still be operating out of Satan's Kingdom. The battleground is in the mind.

Are you going to believe in God and obey Him?

Or are you going to be persuaded by Satan that you do not have to obey God or carry out His commands?

I have been to heaven many times and seen Jesus. (Now more than twenty times.)

However, the most interesting message Jesus gave me was when I was in St. Nicholas Church in Bunbury. The Priest was on a raised platform giving a sermon on a Sunday, and Jesus appeared on the same platform. I was amazed and looked around the congregation, no one else seemed to see Jesus.

Jesus spoke to me, *"Yes, you are correct; only you can see me. I have come to give you a special message. If you obey me, nothing will be impossible for you."*

Jesus spoke to me for maybe 15 minutes before He left, but this is the main point of what He wanted to say. Therefore, I want to repeat this message: ***if you obey Jesus (The Holy Spirit), nothing will be impossible for you***. Jesus said, *"Whatever you ask in my Name, my Father will grant your request."*

However, this is conditional on obeying the commands of Jesus, which are very simple— ***Love the Lord your God with all your heart and love your neighbour as yourself.***

# CHAPTER 1

## The New Holy Spirit Age

This new book of *"The New Holy Spirit Age"* starts here.

The *"New Holy Spirit Age"* revelation started one day when in a home group meeting in 2014, the Holy Spirit led me to say that God had placed signs in the heavens which depicted seasons, times, and ages.

We entered the Water Pourer's age when the Holy Spirit would be poured out on all flesh.

The sign of the Water Pourer signified that the Age of the Holy Spirit was about to start. Just like when a woman is about to give birth, it is very messy and painful, but when the baby is born, the woman forgets her pain and discomfort for the joy that a child has been born into the world. I said this is similar in that the start or birth of the Holy Spirit Age will be very messy and painful, but when the Holy Spirit is poured out on all flesh, there will be joy and celebration, and we will enter a New Golden Age.

At the start of Pisces, the Church age was the end of the Temple and the Law. God was doing a new thing and would save His people thru the sacrifice of Jesus.

So it would be with Aquarius; God would do a new thing.

To explain that each Planetary age was 2,000 years long.

The sign of the Bull from 4,000 BC to 2,000 BC represented the years of Pagan Worship.

The sign of the Ram from 2,000 BC to 0 AD, represented Abraham and the Patriarchs, Substitution of a Ram for Abraham's Sacrifice, Law of Moses and the Law. The Temple and the Sacrificing of a Lamb as forgiveness for sin.

The Fish sign represented 2,000 years of the Age of Jesus as the once and for all sacrifice of sin.

The next day at work, I was given a clear message that the age or time was changing.

A few hours after starting work, I looked at the clock; it said noon mid-day. I did not feel hungry and went and got my lunch. When I returned to my desk, the clock now said 7:30 am, so I put my lunch back in the fridge. Then, I had a meeting, and the clock said 11:00 am, so I went to the room but there was no one there. I went to see my boss, and he said that I was 3 hours early, and it was only 8:00 am.

Then a man came to my desk and asked me the time, the guy sitting next to me told him the time, and the man said, *"No, I am asking Michael what the time is, so I looked at my computer and told him the time."* He looked into my eyes and said, *"Do not forget that you have been told the times are changing. I have never seen that man in my work before. I guess he was an angel."*

When I left work thru a gate, a rotating gate operated with a swipe card. I swiped my card and walked thru the gate. The gate went *click, click, click* very loudly. As I started to walk towards my car, I heard the gate *click!* very loudly, so I turned around to see who was there, but there was no one there. The car park is gravel, so I started to walk towards my car. I heard very loud footsteps in the gravel behind me—a much louder noise than my footsteps, I turned around, and there was no one there. I

# THE NEW HOLY SPIRIT AGE

walked—the footsteps followed me to my car some 300 m away.

I was very glad to get in my car and drove off. It had been an extremely strange day, but I understood this was the Holy Spirit confirming that the age was changing, and the New Holy Spirit Age was commencing soon.

So, I started to think about what this might mean. When Jesus came in the Age of the Fish, the change was very great, the Temple Worship and the Offering of Sacrifices came to an end, and Jesus' death and resurrection were extremely messy—the disciples went thru a terrifying time when their leader was put to death, and they hid away in case they were put to death. However, when Jesus rose from the dead and appeared to them, they were initially amazed and unbelieving, but their doubt would have been changed to unconfined joy. We could not imagine how joyful they were to discover that everything Jesus had told them was true and that He had conquered death and risen again from the dead.

Thus, I started to think about what this might mean for the Age of the Holy Spirit that was about to start. There is no doubt that the Kingdom of Satan has made many gains since the 1970s by destroying the Christian reputation in the world and advancing the Kingdom of Satan. He has made gains in all areas of life, including the Church.

It is not my intention to give glory to Satan as Jesus defeated him at the Cross; it is only a matter of time before God will destroy Satan's Kingdom. "Some Churches" have allowed Satan's worldly philosophies to enter the Church, to change or deny the truth of the Gospel message. To become a Bless–me club that has become irrelevant to people that need the Gospel message, in some instances, a Church without any power over the devil, or so it may appear.

However, God has a plan that is sometimes not obvious, just as it was not obvious to the disciples of Jesus.

This plan is very simple, a new covenant, but this is the covenant:

*I will make with them on those days.*

*I will put my law in their minds and write it on their hearts, I will be their God; they shall be my people, place my laws in their hearts, and remember their sin no more.*

*Moreover, it shall come to pass afterward that I will pour my spirit out on all flesh. Your sons and your daughters shall prophesy.*

*Your old men shall dream; your young men shall see visions and my menservants and maidservants.*

*I will pour out my spirit in those days.*

Some people believe the Age of Pisces the Fish (symbolizes Jesus /Christians) officially Started when Jesus was crucified, rose from the dead, and met with His disciples to eat a fish's meal; 40 days later, He ascended into Heaven.

Some people believe the Age of the Holy Spirit began in 2019.

The Age of Aquarius, the Water Pourer, begins when the March equinox point moves out of the constellation Pisces and into the constellation Aquarius. There is much opinion on the actual date of the start of Aquarius, and there is not a line drawn in the sky between the two planetary systems. I believe the birth of the New Holy Spirit Age has started, but we have not moved into its fullness. I believe it is based on Jesus fulfilling the law at His death and not at the time of His birth. Each covenant God made with man was ratified with death and the shedding of blood.

Therefore, I suggest that each age starts with a sacrifice or death and a new covenant. By saying this, I do not mean that Jesus has to be crucified again, but I am suggesting there will be some event that includes death or sacrifice.

# CHAPTER 2

## The Fullness of the Victory that Jesus Christ Won on the Cross

In January 2020, I was standing in my bathroom after having a shower, and I had just dried myself. I was standing in front of a mirror, and I suddenly heard and felt two blips of liquid land on my feet. When I looked down, I could see two spots of very bright red blood on my feet where you might have expected the nails to have pierced Jesus' feet.

As I looked down, more drops of blood dripped down on my feet, and the drips got quicker until quite a pool of bright red blood surrounded my feet.

I wondered what was happening and became concerned; maybe I was bleeding. I looked over my body, but I could not find any wounds where the blood would be coming from.

When I looked back up into the mirror, I saw Jesus behind me. I continued to look into the mirror as Jesus spoke. He said, *"I am very disappointed with the Church. They are disrespecting me and treating me as if my sacrifice and death on the cross were something of no account; they have no regard for the trauma, the pain, and the excruciating death. They have no real regard or understanding of what it costs me to purchase them to be Children of God. They have no idea of the "Fullness of the Victory" I won for them."*

I understood what he was saying, for the experience, I just had with the blood was very traumatic to think that this bright red blood was seeping out of my body and had formed a pool of blood on the floor.

This experience has so affected me that when I think of it or try to talk about it many times, I will start to weep, especially if the presence of God is very strong.

Then Jesus said, *"Most of the Church are not walking in the "Fullness of the Victory" that I won for them on the cross because the Church is preaching a false Gospel. I am giving you a new commission. I want you to go to churches and speak on the "Fullness of my Victory" and teach the true Gospel."*

He added, *"I will give you the messages to speak."*

After Jesus left, I thought about these things and wondered how these things would come to pass. In a meeting, I was asked to hold in Bunbury Church of Christ in Late January 2020, the Holy Spirit gave me the teaching *"Your Right to be a Child of God."*

This teaching will be one of the mainstays of the Gospel Message.

The teachings eventually came to include:

**Chapter 5.** *Levels of Anointing*
**Chapter 6.** *The Work of the Holy Spirit*
**Chapter 7.** *I call you friends—God's Favour*
**Chapter 8.** *The Body of Christ*
**Chapter 9.** *The Future of the Church*
**Chapter 10.** *The Circumcision Party*

In this New Golden Age, God will make Satan give back everything he stole from us.

Before they left Egypt, God instructed Israel to ask their Egyptian neighbours to give them gold, silver, fine clothes, wealth, etc. God was making Satan pay Israel for everything he had stolen from them while the Egyptians enslaved Israel.

God even required restitution for the Children of Israel that the Egyptians had murdered. Therefore, God will restore everything Satan stole from our bloodline and descendants back to Adam and Eve. This includes death—see *1 Cor 15:29*.

# CHAPTER 3

## Your Right to be a Child of God

**In Summary**

THE GOSPEL MESSAGE IS very simple, and we have made it too complicated:

God's will meant that everything in creation would be subjected to the *Authority of Jesus*.

Those that believe in Jesus are given the *"Gift of Eternal Life."* They have been given the *"Right to become a Child of God."* They are

Children of God; God is their Father, Jesus is their Lord, and the Holy Spirit is their Helper. They are a *"New Creation"* and given the Holy Spirit as *"A Promise."* They have been given a *"New Spirit"* by Jesus coming to live in them. (Born Again) Jesus has paid for all their sins.

They are no longer under the Law and can "Sin No More."

Sin now becomes *to "not believe that Jesus is The Son of God"*. Jesus defeated sin and death and the works of Satan with His blood and sacrifice on the cross. A Child of God is raised to *"Sit in heavenly places in Christ Jesus."*

They have already received the *Gift of Eternal Life*; they cannot lose the *Gift of Eternal Life*; it is a gift. Jesus said, *"He who believes in me shall never die."*

We are a spirit, have a soul (mind), and live in a body.

Our Spirit is the new creation and shall never die and is now living in the heavenly realm.

Our Soul has a carnal or earthly mind with selfish thoughts, emotions, will, and cravings, and is in rebellion with God. Our mind and body need to be transformed into the likeness of Jesus by **obeying the Holy Spirit**.

As Paul said,

> *"Let our minds be transformed into the Mind of Christ. It is no longer I that live but Christ that Lives in Me."*

## In Detail

We receive the *Gift of Eternal Life* by believing in Jesus as the son of God. ***John 3:16***—God so loved the world that He gave His Hon that whoever believes in Him will have eternal life, but condemned whoever does not believe in Jesus.

We receive the Right to be a Child of God.

> ***John 1:2***—Jesus gave those who believe in Him the Right to become Children of God to those who believe in His name—this is the Right to be a Child of God.
>
> ***John 16:8-9***—Jesus said that when the Holy Spirit comes, He will convict the world of Sin, what is Sin, that they do not believe in me.
>
> ***John 14:6***—Jesus said, *"I am the way, the truth, and the life, whoever believes in me will never die, they have already passed from death to life."*

Jesus said, "I would never leave you or forsake you. Whoever comes to me; I will in no way turn away. When I leave, I will return and take you to where I am.

> *John 14:18*—I will not leave you as orphans; I will come to you.

> *2 Corinthians 5:17*—Therefore, if anyone is in Christ, he is a new creation; old things have passed away; behold, all things have become new.

Only believers in Jesus can say Jesus is Lord.

> *1 Corinthians 12:3*—Moreover, no one can say that Jesus is Lord except by the Holy Spirit.

Sons of God are those Led by The Holy Spirit.

> *Romans 8:14*—For as many are led by the Spirit of God; these are sons of God.

If the Holy Spirit Leads you—you are not under the Law.

> ***Galatians 5:18***—But if the Spirit leads you, you are not under the Law.

If we are a Child of God we are seated with Christ in heavenly places.

> ***Ephesians 1 & 2***—Blessed be the God and Father of our Lord Jesus Christ, who has blessed us with every spiritual blessing in the heavenly places in Christ,… and raised us together, and made us sit together in the heavenly places in Christ Jesus.

We have received Jesus and are no longer under the Law.

> ***Romans 8:14***—Jesus was the once and all sacrifice for the forgiveness

of our sins—those led by the Spirit of God are sons of God, for those led by the Holy Spirit, there is no law.

There is now no condemnation for those in Christ Jesus.

There is neither male nor female, Greek nor Jew for those in Christ Jesus.

If you believe Jesus is the Son of God and can confess Jesus as Lord and Saviour, then the Holy Spirit comes and dwells in your heart. He joins with your spirit, you become a New Spiritual Being, a New Spiritual Creation, that has never existed before, and you have received the *Gift of Eternal Life*.

God has raised us to be seated in heavenly places in Christ Jesus. You are already seated in heaven. **We need to pray from heaven to earth, not earth to heaven.**

We are the Body of Christ, and God has placed everything under the feet of Jesus. Therefore, everything has also been placed under our feet. Jesus is in heaven, and if we are his body, we must be seated in heaven also (That is our Spirit).

We have all authority and power over Satan and the devil's works. We have been raised just as Jesus was raised.

We need to understand who we are and that we are made in the image of God. God is Father, Son, and Spirit. We are a spirit; we live in a physical body and have a soul (mind, will, and emotions). Our spirit was dead and then was made alive in Jesus, and we became a new creation, a new being raised with Christ Jesus.

Our spirit was made holy and righteous and cannot sin because the *Righteousness of Jesus* covers us. We are no longer under the Law; those that the Holy Spirit leads are not under the

Law. You cannot lose this *Gift of Eternal Life*. There is nothing you can do to earn eternal life. It was a gift, and you cannot earn a gift by obeying the Law.

Anyone trying to earn the *Gift of Eternal Life* by obeying the Law is trying to destroy the truth of the Sacrifice Jesus made on the cross as the once for all sacrifice for the sins of the whole world. The false gospel says you have to believe in Jesus and obey the Law, and Paul said anyone who preached such a Gospel message would be cursed.

To fully explain your Right to be a Child of God, we need to go back to the beginning.

In the beginning, was the Word, the Word was with God, and the Word was God; He was at the beginning with God. He made all things through Him, and nothing was made that was made without Him.

In Him was Life, and this Life was the light of men. Jesus' title is the Word of God.

> *Revelation 19: Jesus was seated on a white horse leading the armies of God, clothed with a robe dipped in blood, and his name is called The Word of God.*

In Genesis, in the beginning, God created the Heavens and the Earth and the Garden of Eden.

The Garden of Eden was in a heavenly realm, the Lord God created Adam out of the dust of the earth and breathed his Spirit into Adam, and Adam became a spirit being having a soul living in a body. God later created Eve from Adam.

God created man in the image of God. God is Father, Son, and Holy Spirit—a three-part being. I repeat that *we are a spirit, have a soul or mind, and live in a body.*

God walked in the Garden of Eden with Adam and Eve.

In the Garden was the Tree of Life and the Tree of Knowledge of Good and Evil. *The Tree of Life* represents *Jesus*. *The Tree of Knowledge* represents *Satan*.

God said to Adam, *"Of the Tree of Knowledge of Good and Evil, you shall not eat, for you shall surely die on the day you eat of it."*

So, when Adam and Eve ate from the Tree of Knowledge, they did not immediately physically die. However, they died spiritually; their Spirit died and they no longer had a spiritual connection to God.

Death is separation from God. God put Adam and Eve out of the Garden of Eden. He placed an angel at the entrance to the garden so they could not return. The Angel signified that Adam was separated from his divine connection with God.

This also signified that Adam and Eve could not reconnect to God in their current state outside the garden, and they could not eat of the Tree of Life and receive eternal life.

Therefore, every man and woman after Adam and Eve was spiritually dead; their Spirit was dead, and they had no direct connection to God or the heavenly realm. As Paul said, *every human being is dead in their sins—the Sins of Adam and Eve.*

When we confess that we believe that Jesus is the Son of God and when we confess that Jesus is our Lord and Saviour (No man can confess Jesus is Lord except by the Holy Spirit.); then we become a new creation. The Holy Spirit comes and forms a new spirit in us and reconnects our Spirit to God. On that day, we are born again, and as what happened to Jesus, we rise with Him as a new creation. It is no longer I that live but Christ that lives in me.

## THE NEW HOLY SPIRIT AGE

*We are a new creation. We are partakers of the fullness of the victory that Jesus won for us on the cross, and we are seated in heavenly places in Christ Jesus.*

*Our New Spirit has passed from death to life and entered glory with Christ in Heaven. Our Spirit is seated in heaven next to Jesus and is not bound to this earthly realm.*

*There is nothing anyone can do to lose this Gift of Eternal Life. It is a gift from God and is unchangeable once you accept the Gift of believing in Jesus Christ. "And this is the will of Him who sent Me, that everyone who sees the Son and believes in Him may have everlasting life; and I will raise him at the last day."*

God planned that His Son dwells in the whole of creation, and I should submit the whole of creation to the rule and Kingship of Jesus, and we are partakers of that new Spirit in us which is one with Christ Jesus. Christ in us is the *Hope of Glory*.

In the name of Jesus, every knee should bow, and every tongue should confess that **Jesus Christ is Lord to the Glory of God the Father**.

This statement that God so loved the world that He gave His Son Jesus that whoever believed in Him should not perish but have eternal life.

This was a Gift from God. We cannot earn this Gift because Jesus paid the price for our sins. We are reconciled to God the Father thru His Son, Jesus.

Even while we were in our sins, God reconciled us to Himself thru His Son, Jesus. He gave this Gift to every person on this earth. All they have to do to receive the Gift is to acknowledge that **Jesus is the son of God and there is no**

**other name under heaven by which we may be saved.**

Any Gospel message that says we need to believe in Jesus and obey the Law is a false gospel. Paul had harsh words for people who preached such a gospel because they were making the sacrifice of Jesus of no effect. If we can be perfected by obeying the Law, we do not need Jesus. Of course, once you start obeying the Law, you have to obey the whole Law, which is impossible.

The Holy Spirit wants me to tell you that **anyone who believes Jesus is the Christ, the Son of God, is a New Spirit and cannot die.** They have passed from death to life, and their Spirit is already seated in the heavenly places with Christ Jesus.

When we put on Christ, God sees us as Holy and Righteous, and He remembers our sins no more. You cannot lose the *Gift of Eternal*

*Life* when you are a new spiritual being in Jesus. The Holy Spirit comes into our hearts and fuses with our dead Spirit as a surety or promises that we have received eternal life, making us alive in Jesus.

There is nothing you can do to destroy your *Gift of Eternal Life*; a spirit being is eternal, only God can destroy a spirit, and He sees Jesus in you as the sign of righteousness. Only those that do not have the Spirit of Jesus will be destroyed.

You can do nothing to separate yourself from the Love of God, which is in Christ Jesus.

Jesus said that He would send the Holy Spirit, and the Holy Spirit will convict the world of sin, and **sin is when you have not believed in the one and only Son of God—Jesus Christ**.

### *John 16: 7-11*

*Nevertheless, I tell you the truth. It is to your advantage that I go away; if I do not go away, the Helper will not come to you; but I will send him to you if I depart. And when he has come, he will convict the world of Sin, and Righteousness, and of judgment: of Sin, because they do not believe in me; of Righteousness, because I go to My Father and you see me no more; of judgment, because the ruler of this world is judged.*

## Times of Refreshing

### *Acts 3: 19*

*Repent ye therefore, and be converted, that your sins may be blotted out when the times of refreshing shall come from the presence of the Lord. He shall send Jesus Christ, which before was preached unto you: whom the heaven must receive until the times of restitution of all things, which God hath spoken by the mouth of all his holy prophets since the world began.*

For Moses truly said unto the fathers, *"A prophet shall the Lord your God raise unto you of your brethren, like unto me; he shall hear in all things he shall say unto you.*

*Moreover, it shall come to pass that every soul, which will not hear that prophet, shall be destroyed from among the people."*

# CHAPTER 4

## IMPARTATION AND THE LAYING OF HANDS

JEWISH PEOPLE UNDERSTAND THE Impartation of the Holy Spirit and the Hand-laying. In the New Testament, Jesus laid hands on people for healing:

*Luke 13: 10-14*

*Jesus laid his hands on her, and immediately she was made straight and glorified by God.*

The laying of hands was common in the Old Testament, particularly when people dying of old age would want to bless their relatives and lay hands on them and proclaim a blessing.

Therefore, a blessing is normally conveyed by laying hands in the Old Testament.

We have this principle being followed in the life of Moses when God transferred the Holy Spirit to Moses to other people. Either directly by God or normally by the laying of hands.

### *Numbers 11:25*

*Then the Lord came down in the cloud, spoke to him, took of the Spirit upon him, and placed the same upon the seventy elders, and it happened, when the Spirit rested upon them, that they prophesied although they never did so again.*

### Numbers 27:18

*And the Lord said to Moses: "Take Joshua the son of Nun with you, a man in whom is the Spirit, and lay your hand on him."*

### Deuteronomy 34:9

*Now Joshua, the son of Nun, was full of the Spirit of wisdom, for Moses had laid his hands on him; so, the children of Israel heeded him and did as the Lord had commanded Moses.*

So, it can be seen in the Old Testament that the Holy Spirit on Moses was transferred to other people, generally by the laying of hands, and that they received the gifting on Moses as the Holy Spirit directed.

In the New Testament, the laying of hands was a basic principle used in the Church, and it can also be seen that it was not just the Apostles that were laying hands and praying for people:

### Acts 9:17

*Moreover, Ananias went his way and entered the house; and laying his hands on him, he said, "Brother Saul, the Lord Jesus, who appeared to you on the road as you came, has sent me that you may receive your sight and be filled with the Holy Spirit."*

### Hebrews 6:1-3

*Therefore, leaving the discussion of the elementary principles of Christ, let us go on to perfection, not laying again the foundation of repentance from dead works and of faith toward God, 2 of the doctrine of baptisms, of laying of hands, of the resurrection of the dead, and* eternal judgment. 3 And this we will do if God permits.

### 1 Timothy 4:14

*Do not neglect the gift in you, which was given to you by prophecy with the laying on the hands of the eldership.*

### 2 Timothy 1:6

*Therefore, I remind you to stir up the gift of God in you by laying on my hands.*

## My Experiences

I believe it will be useful if I explain my experience of Spiritual Gifts being transferred to me by the laying of hands.

In the experiences below, it will be helpful to explain that John Wimber was converted to Christianity in a Quaker Church. This group of Christians was called Quakers because they shook when the Presence of God came to them.

## (1) Paul Cain—Prophetic Gifting

There were afternoon workshop sessions at a John Wimber conference some years ago. One of these workshops was run by prophet Paul Cain who prayed and laid hands on me.

Paul also spoke prophetically over me about the Spirit of Elijah. That night, I shook under the Anointing of the Holy Spirit that even the bed was shaking and bouncing. I did not sleep that night as God spoke to me about the Office of a Prophet.

I received my Prophetic Office / Anointing from Paul Cain.

## (2) John Wimber—Apostolic Gifting

At a John Wimber conference some years later, the Holy Spirit said to me, *"Be bold and go and ask John Wimber for whatever you want."*

So, I went up to John and asked if I could have a double portion of the Anointing of His

Life. John asked me to sit down and talk with him for a while; then he said, *"The Lord says I am to grant your request."* So, John laid his hands on me and prayed for me to receive the Anointing of His Life.

The effect was dramatic as I shook very strongly, and the chair I was sitting on jumped on its legs, and I felt the power of the Holy Spirit flowing through me very strongly.

I received my Apostolic Office / Anointing from John Wimber. Other Christian leaders have prayed for me, and I have received an impartation from the laying of hands.

I have prayed for many people to receive the Anointing and Gifts. Some of the experiences of these people were life-changing. God used them in ways they had never experienced before.

Some of these people, I also supported and helped in their ministry. It is not my intention that anyone is submitted to me after I pray for them, and they should only ever be submitted to Jesus and the Holy Spirit. Those that the Spirit of God leads are sons of God.

# CHAPTER 5

## Levels of Anointing

Every Christian who gives their life to Jesus receives the Holy Spirit as a promise or confirmation that they are a new creation and have received Jesus into their hearts.

They will know they have been given the right or power to become a Child of God. Many people say they feel different after receiving Jesus as their Lord and Saviour, and this is because they are a new creation.

I believe this is separate from the filling or Baptism of the Holy Spirit. My reason for this is that when Jesus asked Peter who He was, Peter replied that Jesus was Christ, the Messiah.

Jesus replied, *"Blessed are you, Peter, for men did not reveal this to you but my father in heaven."* **No one can say Jesus is Lord except by the Holy Spirit.**

Therefore, Peter was born again right when he confessed to Jesus and received the right to become a Child of God and the promise of the Holy Spirit and the Eternal Life promised in *John 3:16.*

When people ask me, I say I have received the Holy Spirit in me for Eternal Life and the Holy Spirit on me to empower me to do the works of Jesus. Jesus in me is the Hope of Glory, and you shall receive power when the Holy Spirit comes upon you.

There are other levels of Anointing. However, I felt led to focus on these three main levels:

*(1) For Salvation*
*(2) For Power to do Works and Miracles*
*(3) For Authority to Govern*

## Three (3) Levels of God's Anointing

### Old Testament

I am using David as an example.

### (1) Level 1 of the Anointing: For Salvation

> ***1 Samuel 16:13***
>
> *Then Samuel took the horn of oil and anointed him amid his brethren: and the Spirit of the Lord came upon David from that day forward. So, Samuel arose and went to Ramah.*

Every Christian that believes that Jesus is the Son of God receives this level of Anointing. The Holy Spirit is coming and dwelling in people, making them a new creation. Jesus breathed on the disciples and said, *"Receive the Holy Spirit."*

As Paul said, we are the Temple of the Holy Spirit. Christianity is the only religion where God comes and dwells in the person's heart.

## (2) Level 2 of the Anointing: For Power and Works

***1 Samuel 2:4***

*Moreover, the men of Judah came, and there they anointed David king over the house of Judah.*

## (3) Level 3 of the Anointing: For Authority to Govern:

### *2 Samuel 5:3*

*So, all the elders of Israel came to the king in Hebron, and king David made a league with them in Hebron before the Lord: and they anointed David king over Israel.*

## New Testament(1) Level 1 of the Anointing: For Salvation

### *John 20:22*

*Moreover, when he (Jesus) had said this, he breathed on them and said, Receive ye the Holy Spirit.*

## (2) Level 2 of the Anointing: For Power and Works

### *Acts 2:1-4*

*Moreover, when the day of Pentecost fully came, they were all in one accord in one place, and suddenly*

> *there came a sound from heaven like a mighty rushing wind, filling all the house where they were sitting. Moreover, there appeared unto them cloven tongues like as of fire, and it sat upon each of them.*

Moreover, they were all filled with the Holy Ghost and began to speak with other tongues as the Spirit gave them utterance.

## (3) Level 3 of the Anointing: For Authority to Govern

### *Acts 4:31*

> *Moreover, when they had prayed, the place was shaken where they were assembled; they were all filled with the Holy Ghost and boldly spoke God's word.*

I would like to share below *my understanding* of the Three Levels of the Holy Spirit:

## (1) Level 1 of the Anointing: For Salvation

Test every Spirit. It is only by the Holy Spirit that people can say Jesus is their Lord and Saviour.

I have asked many Christians to say Jesus is their Lord and Saviour, but they cannot say Jesus is their Lord and Saviour.

Therefore, it appears that many Christians in churches do not confess Jesus as their Saviour and do not have the First Level of Anointing for Salvation. I have asked priests and bishops to say Jesus is their Lord and Saviour, and they, too, could not.

I estimate that at this point, only 25% of Christians in Western cultures have this level of Anointing.

This is because the Church leaders ensure that the Church members are not filled with the Holy Spirit so that it is easy to control them.

However, recently things are changing, and that old leadership is being removed and replaced with leadership that is more open to the leading of the Holy Spirit. To confirm what I am saying, recently, for 15 months, I went to a church every Sunday. I repeatedly asked if I could hold a meeting on a Friday evening to allow the Holy Spirit to make considerable changes in people's lives. For 15 months, the priest said no, I could not hold the meeting; I eventually left this Church and immediately dreamed that God was turning off the lights in that church because they would not allow the Holy Spirit to move.

I told my friend in that Church about the dream. Two days later, they had an evening meeting in the church, all the lights and power went out, and they had to stop the meeting and leave the building because it was dark. My friend told me that what I had said to him had come true.

This Level 1 of Anointing: For Salvation will teach people and give them guidance, wisdom, and discernment. They can still carry out work for God. Even at level 1, some people can do amazing things for God because of God's Favour.

At any level of the Anointing, the power depends on the relationship and God's Favour. The Holy Spirit is a person, we need to have a relationship with—Jesus through the Holy Spirit.

## (2) Level 2 of the Anointing: For Power and Works

This Level 2 anointing is a life-changing experience where the person becomes a major influence in advancing the Kingdom of Heaven. If we look at the first disciples of Jesus, they were frightened and hid in an upper room until they were Baptized by Fire and the Holy Spirit. They became bold and spoke the Word of God as the Holy Spirit directed them.

As an example, I have an Aboriginal friend named Gloria whom I prayed for in January 2019 to be baptized with fire. In less than a year, Gloria, her husband, and some friends led 1,200 Aboriginals in remote communities to give their lives to Jesus. Moreover, this is just the start of what God will do with someone who is submitted to the Holy Spirit. I estimate Gloria and her team have ministered to more than 3,000 people.

## (3) Level 3 of the Anointing: For Authority to Govern

This Level 3 anointing is for Authority to Rule on the earth on behalf of God.

David had this Level of Anointing when he was King over the whole of Israel.

Moses also had this anointing when he was the leader of Israel. Joshua also had this level of Anointing when he led Israel into the Promised Land.

Moses laid hands on Joshua and gave him this gift of Wisdom and Authority to rule Israel on behalf of God.

It is interesting that when people in the Bible have this Authority to Rule on God's behalf and people rebel against that person or authority, then the people die. It is because they have not rebelled against Moses but against God.

**My Experiences with the Levels of Anointing**

**(1) Level 1 of the Anointing: For Salvation**

There was a seven-week course, a Saints Alive Course, in an Anglican Church in Bunbury, WA, where they prayed for you to receive the Holy Spirit at the end of the course. This was receiving the Holy Spirit from people praying for me by Laying of Hands. There was a problem though. As I had been fasting for 3 days and wanted the gift of speaking in tongues, I did not receive the gift of speaking in tongues when they prayed for me.

Some 3 days later, during my lunch break at work, God told me I could not earn the gift by fasting, which was a Gift.

So, while kneeling on a beach in a quiet place near my work at lunchtime, the power of God came to me, and I fell over. The power of the Holy Spirit came on me so strongly that I could not get up for 2 hours or more. I spoke in tongues and was led thru alternating sessions of weeping, repentance, and thanking God.

At the end of the session, I was so weak I could hardly walk, I went back to my work and then went home early. I was so weak and tired that I slept until the next day.

## (2) Level 2 of the Anointing: For Power and Works The Baptism of Fire of the Holy Spirit

I felt led by the Holy Spirit that I needed the Baptism of Fire of the Holy Spirit. The Holy Spirit told me that the Baptism of the Holy Spirit and the Baptism of Fire were two separate events. I had never heard of such teaching.

So, I prayed and fasted over many months to be baptized in the Fire of the Holy Spirit. One day, I was invited to a Pastor's house in Capel, and a prophet named Brian Anderson was staying with him. Brian was recognized as a prophet in the Uniting Church. I went to the house in Capel around 7:00 pm. A group of people listened to Brian, including me, giving personal testimonies about how God had mightily used him.

The Holy Spirit said, *"Be Bold and ask for whatever you want."*

So, I asked Brian, *"Can I have a double portion of the Anointing on your life?"* Brian was taken aback and stopped speaking. I could see he was praying, then he said, *"What you want is the Baptism of Fire."*

So, around 7:30 pm, he laid his hands on me and prayed for me to receive the Baptism of Fire of the Holy Spirit. I started to shake, and then I felt like I was burning. The burning sensation got worse and worse; my forehead and hands were the worst but generally all over.

I felt as if I was about to die and prayed to God if the burning sensation could be less severe as it was killing me, and the burning sensation got less but was still only bearable.

So, I was standing in the lounge and went into what I can only describe as a vision—where Jesus came and spoke to me, but I did not believe I was in the room anymore. I had no sense of time, so when things started to calm down and came to myself, I found I was in a dark room on my own. I heard talking and saw the light from the kitchen.

I went to the kitchen where Brian and some people still gathered. I said, *"That was not very polite to leave me there on my own."*

They replied that they had waited for me but had gotten fed up and gone to the kitchen. I had been in the room for nearly 5 hours, and it was now past midnight. I found it hard to believe I had been standing in a room for 5 hours, but I still felt burning all over and had met Jesus, so I could see by the clock in the kitchen that what they said was true.

I drove from Capel to my Home in Bunbury, some 20 minutes by car. While driving along, I saw a bright green star in the sky ahead. The green star got nearer and nearer and lower. I felt it was going to hit my car, so I braked quite sharply, and the star hit the ground about 12 feet in front of my car and disappeared.

At the same time, I heard an audible voice that said, *"I saw Satan fall like a star from heaven."* I looked around to see who had spoken, but I could not see anyone.

The burning sensations went on for 4 or more days, particularly with flames on the palms of my hands which I could see, and a burning sensation in the middle of my forehead. I later understood the reason behind the words, as I had been given the authority to perform many amazing works as the Holy Spirit instructed me.

Within a very short time, I prayed with 400 to 500 people to give their lives to Jesus and prayed for them to be filled with the Holy Spirit. Also, the people I prayed for were healed of diseases, even incurable diseases.

Sometimes the healings were instantaneous, and other times they took longer.

## (3) Level 3 of the Anointing: For Authority to Govern

I have to say that I believe I do not have Level 3. I have prayed for a very small number of people to receive level 3.

I have a certain authority that, at certain times, I receive whatever I ask for if the Holy Spirit has instructed me to ask.

I feel the answer to why I have not experienced level 3 is very simple—I have not cultivated a strong enough relationship with the Father.

This is a safety mechanism for why I have not received Level 3.

People who move to Level 3 have much higher accountability and expectation from God.

They need a very strong relationship with God, or they will die at this level of Anointing. Anyone who lightly treats this Level 3 of anointing will not live long.

There have been very many of God's Servants who died when they used their authority with contempt for God's Authority.

When the Third Level of Anointing is present, even lying to God can cause instant death. In the Old Testament, when Uzzah put out his hand to touch the Ark of God, he died.

### 2 Samuel 5:3

*So, all the elders of Israel came to the king in Hebron, and king David made a league with them in Hebron before the Lord: and they anointed David king over Israel.*

David now has all Authority and Power over the whole of Israel.

In the Book of Acts, level 3, Authority to Govern took place in ***Acts Chapter 4***.

> ²³ *And being let go, they went to their companions and reported what all the chief priests and elders said.* ²⁴ *So when they heard that, they raised their voice to God with one accord and said: "Lord, you are God, who made heaven and earth and the sea, and all that is in them,* ²⁵ *who [c]by the mouth of your servant David have said: 'Why did the nations rage, Moreover, the people plot vain things?* ²⁶ *The kings of the earth took their stand, And the rulers were gathered together Against the Lord and His Christ.'* ²⁷ *"For truly against Your holy Servant Jesus, whom you anointed, both Herod and Pontius Pilate, with the Gentiles and the people of Israel, were gath-*

> *ered together* [28] *to do whatever, your hand and your purpose determined before to be done.* [29] *Now, Lord, look on their threats, and grant to Your servants that with all boldness they may speak your word,* [30] *by stretching out your hand to heal and that signs and wonders may be done through the name of your holy servant Jesus."* [31] *And when they had prayed, the place where they were assembled was shaken; they were all filled with the Holy Spirit and spoke the word of God with boldness.*

In ***Acts Chapter 5***, we can see the effect of this Authority to Govern Level 3 Anointing Shortly after this, Ananias and Sapphira lied to Peter and fell dead, and great fear came upon the Church. Great fear also came from the ordinary people in the Temple. Multitudes were added to the new Church.

## Acts 5:12-16

*12 And through the hands of the Apostle, many signs and wonders were done among the people. Moreover, they were all with one accord in Solomon's Porch. 13, Yet none of the rest dared join them, but the people esteemed them highly. 14 And believers were increasingly added to the Lord, multitudes of both men and women, 15 so that they brought the sick out into the streets and laid them on beds and couches, that at least the shadow of Peter passing by might fall on some of them. 16 Also, a multitude gathered from the surrounding cities to Jerusalem, bringing sick people and those tormented by unclean spirits, and they were all healed.*

I want to impart some comments about Baptism. God is one but has three parts, Father, Son, and Holy Spirit.

There is One Baptism, yet One Baptism also has three parts reflecting God's three personalities or natures.

**(1) Water** – ***Repentance—Gift of Eternal Life*** – *Right to enter the outer court of Temple*

**(2) Spirit** – ***Communion with God*** – *Right to enter the inner court of Temple*

**(3) Fire** – ***Presence of God*** – *Right to enter into the Holy of Holies (Through the Blood of Jesus)*

## Authorization from God to Baptize at Different Levels

Acts show that Philip was an evangelist who did many miracles. Philip baptized people in water in the name of Jesus.

# THE NEW HOLY SPIRIT AGE

Acts says they did not receive the Holy Spirit; the Apostles Peter and John had to come and lay hands on people to receive the Holy Spirit. It appears that some people are:

- **Authorized to Baptize in Water**
- **Authorized to Baptize in Holy Spirit**
- **Authorized to Baptize in Fire**
- **Authorized for higher levels of Anointing—**
- **Seven Spirits of God**
- **Authorized for Spirit of Elijah**
- **Authorized for Spirit of Moses** (Moses and Elijah were at Jesus' Transfiguration—these are the two Lampstands that Stand before God.)

I am authorized to pray for people to become an apostle, a prophet, an evangelist, a pastor, and a teacher.

It is worth mentioning that some people can be filled directly with the Holy Spirit from Heaven, but this is not currently the normal way God imparts the Holy Spirit to people. Normally, someone lays hands on you and prays for you to be filled with the Holy Spirit.

## Methods of Being Filled/Baptized with the Holy Spirit

### *Acts 8:14-19*

*Now when the apostles which were at Jerusalem heard that Samaria had received the word of God, they sent unto them Peter and John. Who, when they came down, prayed for them, that they might receive the Holy Ghost:*

*(For as yet he was fallen upon none of them: only they were baptized in the Name of the Lord Jesus.) And when Simon saw that through laying on of the apostles' hands the Holy Ghost was given, he offered them money,*

### Acts 10:34-46

*Then Peter opened his mouth and said, of a truth, I perceive that God is no respecter of persons:*

*However, every nation that feared him and worketh righteousness is accepted by him. The word which God sent unto the children of Israel, preaching peace by Jesus Christ: (he is Lord of all).*

*That word, I say, ye know, which was published throughout all Judaea, and began from Galilee, after the Baptism which John preached;*

*How God anointed Jesus of Nazareth with the Holy Ghost and with power: who went about doing good and healing all that were oppressed of the devil; for God was with him.*

*Moreover, we are witnesses of all things which he did both in the land of the Jews and Jerusalem; whom they slew and hanged on a tree:*

*Him God raised on the third day and showed him openly; Not to all the people, but unto witnesses chosen before God, even to us, who did eat and drink with him after he rose from the dead.*

*Moreover, he commanded us to preach unto the people and testify that it is he who was ordained of God to be the Judge of the quick and dead. To him, give all the prophets witness that whosoever believeth in him shall receive remission of sins through his name.*

*While Peter yet speaks these words, the Holy Ghost fell on all of them who heard the word. Moreover, they of the circumcision which believed were astonished, as many as came with Peter, because that on the Gentiles also was poured out the gift of the Holy Ghost, for they heard them speak with tongues and magnify God.*

In the New Testament, it was normal for God to convey this blessing of the Holy Spirit by the Laying of the Apostle's hands. Of course, God can directly convey a blessing on the Day of Pentecost. The Pentecost and the first outpouring of the Holy Spirit on the Gentiles were special occasions. It was normal after those events for people to receive the Holy Spirit through the Laying of Hands and Prayer.

This resulted in the person being filled with the Holy Spirit and receiving the Gifts of the Holy Spirit.

# CHAPTER 6

## The Work of the Holy Spirit

**The Work of the Holy Spirit has three parts:**

(1) **The Holy Spirit in You—***Christ in You is the Hope of Glory*—The Right to be a Child of God

(2) **The Holy Spirit on You**—The Power to do the works God has prepared for you.

## (3) The Holy Spirit thru You—*Jesus is the Spirit of Prophecy*—Speaking the Word of God

Jesus most clearly defined the work of the Holy Spirit.

In the Gospel of John, Jesus spoke about the Holy Spirit many times, he defined the work of the Holy Spirit, but it is spread over many chapters and is sometimes difficult to understand.

Therefore, I have summarized the scriptures here and will explain the work of the Holy Spirit under the three headings above.

### *John 1: 12*

*However, as many received him, he gave them the right to be Children of God.*

### John 3: 3-8:

*Jesus said to Nicodemus - unless one is born again, he cannot see the kingdom of God, unless you are born of water and the Spirit, you cannot enter the kingdom of God, that which is born of the flesh is flesh, that which is born of the Spirit is Spirit, do not marvel that I say to you must be born again. The wind blows where it wishes, and so is everyone born of the Spirit.*

### John 4:23-24

*However, the Hour is coming when true worshippers will worship the Father in Spirit and truth, for the Father is seeking such to worship him. God is Spirit, and those who worship him must worship in Spirit and truth.*

### *John 6:62-64*

*It is the Spirit who gives life; the flesh profits nothing. The words I speak to you are Spirit, and they are life.*

### *John 7:38*

*Out of his heart, he who believes in me will flow rivers of living water. However, he spoke concerning the Spirit whom those believing in Him would receive.*

### *John 10:27-29*

*My sheep hear my voice, and I know them, and they follow me. Moreover, I give them eternal life; they shall never perish; neither shall anyone snatch them out of my hand. My Father who has given them to me is greater than all, and no one can snatch them out of My Father's hand. My Father and I are one.*

### John 10:37-38

*If I do not do the works of My Father, do not believe me, but if I do, though you do not believe in me, believe the works that you may know the Father is in me and I in him.*

### John 13:20

*He who receives whomever I send receives Me, and he who receives me receives the him who sent me.*

### John 14:6

*I am the way, the truth, and the life. No one comes to the Father except through me.*

### *John 14:12*

*I say to you that he who believes in me shall do the works I will do and that the Father is glorified in the Son. If you ask anything in my name, I will do it.*

### *John 14:16*

*I will pray to the Father, and he will give you another Helper that He may abide with you forever, the Spirit of Truth whom the world cannot receive because it neither sees him nor knows him, but you know him for he dwells with you and will be in you.*

### *John 15:7*

*If you abide in me and my words abide in you. You will ask what you desire, and it shall be done for you.*

## *John 15:23*

*If anyone loves me, he will keep my word, and my Father will come to him and make our home with him.*

## *John 15:26*

*When the Helper comes, whom I shall send to you from the Father, the Spirit of truth who proceeds from the Father, he will testify of me.*

## *John 16:7-14*

*It is to your advantage that I go away: if I do not go away, the Helper will not come, but if I depart, I will send him to you, and when he has come. He will convict the world of sin, righteousness, and judgment.*

*Of sin because they do not believe in me; of righteousness, because I go to my Father; of judgment because the ruler of this world is judged.*

*However, when the Spirit of truth has come, He will guide you into all truth; for He will not speak on his authority, but whatever He hears, He will speak; and tell you things to come.*

*He will glorify Me, for He will take what is mine and declare it to you.*

### *John 17:2-3*

*You have given him authority over all flesh that he should give eternal life to as many as you have given him. Moreover, this is eternal life that they may know you, the only true God and Jesus Christ you have sent.*

***Acts 1: 8***

*You shall receive power when the Holy Spirit has come upon you.*

***Acts 2:1-4***

*When the day of Pentecost had fully come, they were all in one accord in one place. Moreover, a sound from heaven came suddenly like a mighty rushing.*

***Revelation 19:10***

*Worship God! For the testimony of Jesus is the Spirit of prophecy.*

## (1) The Holy Spirit in You

The Holy Spirit in you was covered in *Chapter 5: Your Right to be a Child of God*. When we believe that Jesus is the Son of God, this is the work of the Holy Spirit.

No man can say, *"Jesus is Lord except by the Holy Spirit" (1 Cor 12:3)*. Then the Holy Spirit comes into you and changes your dead Spirit into a new creation in Christ Jesus. You have become a new creation, a new spiritual being. The Holy Spirit has merged with your Spirit and forms part of this new creation, Jesus in you, the hope of Glory.

This is the *Born Again* experience that Jesus explained to Nicodemus. Every Christian who says Jesus is their Lord and Saviour has been born again and received the gift of eternal life.

They have the Holy Spirit in them as the surety and the promise that they are Children of God.

Jesus said, *"To those who believe in me, I will give them the Right (or Power) to be a Child of God. The Kingdom of God is within you."*

The work of the Holy Spirit is to lead us and make known God's will for our life. As it is written, **those led by the Spirit of God are Sons of God.**

We are no longer under the Law when led by the Holy Spirit. There is now no condemnation for those in Christ Jesus—*Romans Chapter 8.*

## (2) The Holy Spirit on You

The Holy Spirit on you is to empower you to carry out good works that God prepared for you from the earth's foundation. In the *Book of Acts*, the Holy Spirit on you is recorded *three* times:

1. Jesus breathed on the disciples and said receive the Holy Spirit.

2. Jesus said to wait, and you shall receive power when the Holy Spirit comes upon you. This was the Day of Pentecost when the Holy Spirit came in a mighty rushing wind, and

3. When the council of the High Priest released Peter and John, they went to their companions and reported all the high Priest had said. Then they raised their voice to God in one accord, and when they had prayed, the place where they were assembled was shaken, and they were all filled with the Holy Spirit, and they spoke the word of God with boldness.

When we want to carry out the works of God, it is very simple. We become like little children—we listen to the Holy Spirit and obey his instructions. When we do that, we are not the ones who do the works, but the Holy Spirit does them. **The Holy Spirit will give us the power we need to carry out the works.** It is a complete waste of time to do any work when the Holy Spirit has not instructed us.

## (3) The Holy Spirit, thru you

Jesus is the "Word of God." Jesus is the Spirit of Prophecy.

The Old Testament says that the Lord's Word came to Moses, Elijah, Elisha, Isaiah, Jeremiah, Ezekiel, Jonah, Hosea, Amos, Micah, Zephaniah Haggai, Zechariah, and Malachi. Other prophets said the burden of the Lord or Thus says the Lord.

Therefore, God spoke through the prophets in the Old Testament.

In the New Testament, Jesus said that one of the works of the Holy Spirit was to speak through the disciples, and they would speak as the Holy Spirit instructed them.

Speaking the Word of God is associated with power. When the prophets spoke or prayed, amazing power of God was displayed. This included all the wonders in Egypt to deliver the people of Israel from Pharaoh, calling down fire in the test between Elijah and the prophets of Baal.

When one prophet spoke in the Old Testament, the power of his words caused the altar to be broken in two, and the ashes and offerings fell onto the floor.

Even in the New Testament, many powerful miracles happened when the Apostles and disciples spoke the word of God as the Holy Spirit instructed them.

When a prophet speaks in Church, you can feel his power and authority in his words.

There are *three types of Prophets*:

1. **A true prophet of God**. He speaks as directed by the Holy Spirit.

2. **A mistaken Prophet**. He thinks God has spoken, but God did not instruct him to speak. (Maybe the message

was personal only for the prophet) (God will protect this person.)

3. **A False Prophet.** He says God has spoken to him when he knows he is lying and God did not speak to him. This type of prophet is trying to make a reputation for himself. Or destroy someone. *Any prophet who deliberately speaks lies will surely die—refer to the Old Testament.* I know two people who died after speaking lies and saying what God said when he did not.

# CHAPTER 7

# I Call You Friends—God's Favour

IN THIS CHAPTER, I suggest that if you have God's Favour, you are no longer constrained by your position in the Kingdom of God.

We know that Jesus had trusted disciples who were much closer to him than other disciples. We know many followers of Jesus, yet the Disciples of Jesus had a much closer relationship than the other followers.

Jesus revealed many things to His disciples that He did not reveal to his followers. I suggest that if you have God's Favour, you will be persecuted by some Christians, and these Christians see you as a threat and are jealous of your favour.

### *John 12:15*

*My commandment is that you love one another as I have loved you. Greater love has no one than to lay down one's life for his friends. You are my friends if you do whatever I command you no longer do I call you servants, for a servant, does not know what his master is doing; but I have called you friends, for all things that I heard from my Father I have made known to you.*

*We have to look at what happened before this to put this in context. Before this, Jesus' disciples had been with him from the beginning—for three and a half years; they had faithfully supported the Ministry of Jesus.*

Other followers had left Jesus. When Jesus said they had to eat his body and drink his blood, all the followers said this was too hard and left Jesus, except the Disciples. Jesus asked his disciples if they would leave, and they responded, *"You are the Christ; you have the words of Eternal Life; where else can we go."*

The Disciples had supported Jesus' ministry against all opposition and peer pressure, and they had forsaken all to follow him and were willing to give up things of the world to follow and support the Kingdom of God. When we have a love and passion for Jesus and the Kingdom of God, which is all-consuming until all we want is Jesus, **we will have God's Favour.**

God's Favour is not a formula; it is based on relationship, and our Authority and Power in the Holy Spirit are based on our relationship with Jesus. When we have a relationship, we have God's Favour; we have Power and Authority because Jesus goes with us, and the Holy Spirit is with us.

Was it the shadow of Peter that healed the sick? Or was it the shadow of Jesus walking with Peter?

Jesus said:

### *John 6:53-69*

*Then Jesus said to them, "Most assuredly, I say to you that you have no life in you unless you eat the flesh of the Son of Man and drink His blood. Whoever eats my flesh and drinks my blood has eternal life, and I will raise him on the last day. My flesh is the food, and my blood is the drink.*

*He who eats my flesh and drinks my blood abides in me, and I in him. As the living Father sent me, and I live because of the Father, he who feeds on me will live because of me. This is the bread which came down from heaven—not as your fathers ate the manna and are dead. He who eats this bread will live forever."*

These are the things He said in the synagogue as He taught in Capernaum. Many Disciples turned away, therefore, when they heard this, many of his disciples said, *"This is a hard saying; who can understand it?"*

When Jesus knew in himself that His Disciples complained about this, He said to them, *"Does this offend you? What if you should see the Son of Man ascend where he was before? It is the Spirit who gives life; the flesh profits nothing. The words that I speak to you are Spirit and life. However, some of you do not believe."*

For Jesus knew from the beginning who they were who did not believe and would betray Him. Moreover, He said, *"Therefore I have said to you that no one can come to me unless it has been granted to him by my father."*

Many of His Disciples went back and walked with Him no more from that time. Then Jesus said to the twelve, *"Do you also want to go away?"* However, Simon Peter answered, *"Lord, to whom we shall go? You have the words of eternal life. Also, we have come to believe and know that you are the Christ, the Son of the living God."*

### John 26: 27

*However, when the helper comes, whom I shall send to you from the Father, the Spirit of truth who proceeds from the Father, he will testify of me. Moreover, you also will bear witness because you have been with me from the beginning.*

The Disciple John had great Favour with Jesus, and the other Disciples recognized this. He was known as the Disciple that Jesus loved. Peter motioned John to ask Jesus a difficult question because he knew Jesus would give him the answer because of his relationship with Jesus.

### Do we have such a relationship?

### John 13:21-26

*When Jesus had said these things, He was troubled in Spirit and testified and said, "Most assuredly, I say to you, one of you will betray me." Then the disciples looked at one another, perplexed about whom he spoke.*

There was leaning on Jesus' blossom, one of His Disciples whom Jesus loved. Simon Peter, therefore, motioned to him to ask who it was of whom He spoke.

Then, leaning back on Jesus' breast, he said to Him, *"Lord, who is it?"* Jesus answered, *"It is he to whom I shall give a piece of bread when I have dipped it."* And having dipped the bread, He gave it to Judas Iscariot, the Son of Simon.

**Three Disciples were given more Favour than the others. Jesus singled out Peter, James, and John for special treatment**.

**Mathew 17:1-8: The Transfiguration of Jesus**

After six days, Jesus took Peter, James, and John, his brother, and led them up on a high mountain by themselves; he was transfigured before them. His face shone like the sun, and his clothes became as white as the light. Moreover, behold, Moses and Elijah appeared to them, talking with Him.

Then Peter answered and said to Jesus, *"Lord, it is good for us to be here; if you wish, let us make here three tabernacles: one for you, one for Moses, and one for Elijah."*

While he was still speaking, a bright cloud overshadowed them; suddenly, a voice came out of the cloud, saying, *"This is my beloved Son, in whom I am well pleased. Hear Him!"*

Moreover, when the Disciples heard it, they fell on their faces and were greatly afraid. However, Jesus came and touched them and said, *"Arise, and do not be afraid."* When they had lifted their eyes, they saw no one but Jesus only.

We know that God's Favour supersedes our position in the Kingdom of God; because of David's relationship with God, he was able to do something that was not lawful, that is, to take the showbread and eat it, something that was not lawful for anyone but a priest to do.

## Luke 6:3-5

*However, Jesus answering them said, "Have you not even read this, what David did when he was hungry, he and those who were with him: how he went into the house of God, took and ate the showbread, and also gave some to those with him, which is not lawful for any but the priests to eat?" Moreover, he said to them, "The Son of Man is also Lord of the Sabbath."*

Because of David's relationship with God, God gave him amazing Favour, making him King and killing Goliath. David was given the grace to subdue all his enemies and give Israel peace. Even though David's conduct was not perfect, God gave David amazing Favour.

If we look at Joseph, he was given a dream and amazing Favour by God, eventually becoming co-ruler of Egypt and almost equal to Pharaoh.

I want to say that those who have great Favour will also receive great persecution, and this will be because of jealousy and hatred. The mindset is that God is not fair; *why is this person blessed, and I am not blessed?* They do not understand that the person has a special relationship with God and that Favour depends on the relationship.

Thus, David was persecuted by Saul. Many times, Saul tried to kill David. David's brothers did not like David because of his Favour from God.

His brothers also persecuted Joseph because they hated that he was their father's favourite.

Those with God's Favour will often be hated, put in a pit, sold into slavery, have their reputation slandered, and put in prison.

However, God's Favour is unstoppable, so eventually, he will raise them to the highest position.

Many years ago, I had an interesting experience confirming that you would be persecuted if you had God's Favour. I spoke the Gospel to a man in my workplace. He gave his life to Jesus and invited him to come to my Church. Before this, he was an atheist.

One Christmas, as was the custom, the Church was given an empty shop in a shopping mall to collect food, gifts, and money to make up Christmas Hampers. This man was given the job of being in charge of the Shop and the Christmas Hamper program. With only approximately two weeks to Christmas, I visited him at the Shop and asked how the Christmas Hamper Program was going.

He was very angry and negative. He said he had only received a few tins of food on the shelves over the last couple of weeks and less than 20 dollars in cash. I said that I would pray about it. His reaction was interesting as he became quite angry.

I said I would pray anyway and then forgot about it. Straight after Christmas, he testified that they had collected and distributed a large number of Christmas Hampers and also were able to give away hundreds of dollars to help needy families. After Church at Morning Coffee, I said what a fantastic job he had done, and then I reminded him that I said I would pray.

His reaction was not what I was expecting. He swore at me, saying, *"Who do you think you are? Do you think you are better than me? Do you think your prayers are better than mine?*

Thus, I was very taken aback but puzzled by what he said; maybe it was true. *Did I think I was better than him?*

So, I asked the Holy Spirit, *"Surely I am not better than anyone else that my prayers are answered, and their prayers are not."*

The Holy Spirit answered, consider the situation where you need a great Favour and ask three people to grant your Favour.

***Firstly, you go to a person you hardly know** and ask them to grant you your favour.* They'd reply, *"I do not think so, I hardly know you."*

***Secondly, you go to someone you know moderately well.*** You ask them if they can grant your favour. They'd reply, *"I sort of know you, but I am very busy, so I might not get to answer your request."*

***Thirdly, you go to your very best friend.*** He'd say, *"Of course, I will grant you this favour. I would do anything for you because you are my best friend."*

So, with those who have God's Favour, God will answer your prayer request when other people do not get an answer because they do not have a relationship. In the Old Testament, God implemented a Covenant with people to show they had a relationship, and God was initially known as the God of Abraham, Isaac, and Jacob.

Once in a church of approximately 60-70 people, the Holy Spirit instructed me to tell the congregation that we would stand and wait in silence on the Holy Spirit for 5 minutes, and they would receive a blessing from God.

As we stood, the Holy Spirit revealed to me what the people were thinking. One person thought, *"This Holy Spirit business is a complete load of rubbish."* Another person thought, *"I hope this is not going to take long as I have a game of golf at 11:00."* Another thought, *"When I get home, I have to cook the dinner, it is good that*

*I have already prepared the vegetables and saved time."* And so on and on it went...

This waiting was at the end of the service, so at the end of the 5 minutes, many people walked off muttering and complaining to each other.

Only 3 people came to me and said it was the most amazing experience ever.

The point I am making is that if you have God's Favour, you will have religious experiences. If you do not have any Favour with God or do not expect anything to happen, that is what you will receive because the Kingdom of God operates on faith.

Therefore, you will receive exactly what you believe you will receive. Many people do not receive anything from God because that is their expectation. People who have God's Favour and a relationship with God will receive more and more because that is their expectation.

People who do not have a relationship with God will receive very little because that is their expectation. They will persecute the people who have God's Favour because it seems very unfair that one person seems to have lots of Godly experiences and blessings, yet they have none. They see this as God being very unfair, and that is why it appears that God's Favour is not fair.

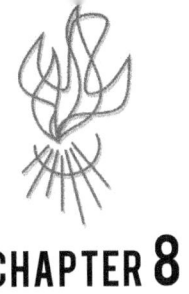

# CHAPTER 8

## The Body of Christ

IN THE BODY OF Christ, everyone is supposed to have a ministry.

> **Apostle**
> **Prophet**
> **Evangelist**
> **Pastor**
> **Teacher**
> **Other Ministries**

(e.g., Administration, Finance, Hospitality, Children, Cleaning, Distribution to Widows, etc.)

## The purpose of the Church is to bring Glory to God by:

### *Mark 16:*

*Go into all; The world and preach the Gospel. And these signs shall follow those that believe in my name. They will cast out demons, speak in new tongues, and take up serpents; if they drink anything deadly, it shall not harm them. They will lay hands on the sick, and they shall recover.*

## The Church has a God-ordained Structure:

### *Ephesians 4: 11-16*

*Moreover, he gave some to be Apostles, some Prophets, some Evangelists, and some pastors and teachers, for the equipping of the saints for the work of ministry, for the edifying of the body of Christ, till we all come to the unity of the faith and the knowledge of the Son of God, to a perfect man, to the measure of the stature of the fullness of Christ; that we should no longer be children, tossed to and fro and carried about with every wind of doctrine, by the trickery of men, in the cunning craftiness of deceitful plotting; but, speaking the truth in love, may grow up in all things into him who is the head—Christ—from whom the whole body, joined and knit together by what every joint supplied, the effective working by which every part does its share, causes growth of the body for the edifying of itself in love.*

## *1 Corinthians 12: 28-31*

*Now you are the body of Christ and members individually. Moreover, God has appointed these in the Church: first Apostles, second Prophets, third Teachers, after that miracle, gifts of healing, help, administrations, and varieties of tongues. Are all Apostles? Are all Prophets? Are all Teachers? Are all workers of miracles? Do all have gifts of healing? Do all speak with tongues? Do all interpret? However, earnestly desire the best gifts. However, I will show you a more excellent way.*

**The Church should function with everyone participating and contributing to the service. Some people are to prophesy. Some people are to have a Psalm; some people are to give teachings, some are to give revelations, some speak in tongues, some interpret,**

**and some speak as the spirit leads them to improve.**

**The Gift of Prophecy is subject to the Prophets.**

*1 Corinthians 14: 26-32*

*How is it then, brethren? Whenever you come together, you have a psalm, teaching, a tongue, a revelation, and an interpretation. Let all things be done for edification. If anyone speaks in a tongue, let there be two or three, each in turn, and let one interpret. However, if there is no interpreter, let him keep silent in Church and speak to himself and God. Let two or three prophets speak, and let the others, judge. However, let the first keep silent if anything is revealed to another sitting by. You can all prophesy one by one that all may learn and*

> *all may be encouraged. Moreover, the spirits of the prophets are subject to the prophets. God is not the author of confusion but peace, as in all the churches of the saints.*

God's Church is supposed to function when the Apostle/Prophet is in charge. When Israel was led out of Egypt, the prophet was God's representative; the priest was there to carry out the directions of the Prophet.

It was Moses who was God's representative, not Aaron.

The Prophet's function (Moses) was to listen to the Instructions of God and relay them to the people and the Priest.

On several occasions when people rebelled and rose against Moses, God's punishment was sometimes very severe.

Miriam was struck down with Leprosy when she complained against Moses regarding the wife that he had married.

In *"The Korah Rebellion against Moses and Aaron,"* it is important to note that the people were killed not for their rebellion against Moses, but because Moses was God's representative, the people were rebelling against God. God was very displeased.

### *Numbers 16: 1–50*

*Korah, Dothan, Eleazar, and 250 Elders of the Children of Israel gathered against Moses and Aaron. They would not recognize Moses' authority. Moses replied that the next day God would show who his representative was.*

He told the 250 elders to take censors and put fire and incense in the censors and present themselves before the Lord. The Glory of the

Lord appeared over Israel; Moses led the people to the Tents of Korah, Dothan, and Eleazar; Moses said, *"By this, you shall know that the Lord has sent me to do all these works, for I have not done them of my own will."*

Then the ground opened up and swallowed all the tents and the household of Korah, Dothan, and Eleazar, and fire came out from the Lord and consumed the two hundred and fifty men offering incense. The next day the people complained and rebelled against Moses and Aaron again, and those who died in the plague were fourteen thousand seven hundred, besides those who died in the Korah incident.

I was listening to a YouTube video of a well-known pastor.

He said he did not allow prophets to speak in his Church. The reason he gave was that he was afraid that the prophets would speak things that were not true and bring confusion and division to his Church.

My immediate thoughts on this statement were:

1. ***He does not know the authority and power he has as a Child of God.***

2. ***If he is afraid, he does not know Jesus—perfect love casts out all fear.*** Fear is a symptom of the Kingdom of Satan, **and *there is no fear for those in Christ Jesus.*** We have the spirit of boldness and a sound mind.

3. ***He does not understand how the Church is to operate.*** All prophetic utterance in the Church is subject to the Prophets.

If one Prophet gets up and speaks, the other prophets are to weigh what has been said and confirm if it is from God or not.

4. ***Some of the people in his Church are not filled with the Holy Spirit.*** If they were filled with the Holy Spirit, immediately after the Prophet spoke, the Holy Spirit in the believer would confirm if the prophecy was from God or the Holy Spirit would deny the prophecy and say this is not the Word of God. So, if his congregation is easily confused, they have a major problem.

I want to state very clearly that many of the Pastors on YouTube are from God. I and anyone else do not have the authority to judge someone else as being from God or not. There is only one test: ***Can the person say Jesus is their Lord and Saviour?***

My experience with some priests and pastors is that when I asked them to say *"Jesus is their Lord and Saviour,"* they could not say this. However, we have the gift of discernment, and if they say it is from the Holy Spirit, we will have that inner knowing and peace if what they are saying is from God.

Many years ago, within 6 weeks of my wife being converted to become a Christian, the pastor of the Church we attended came to our house complained that my wife was unwilling to be subject to the church leadership. (They insisted she was going to hell if she was not baptized and speaking in tongues.)

She (only being a Christian for 6 weeks) asked the pastor to say, *"Jesus was his Lord and Saviour,"* but he could not. He became very angry and, with swearing, banned us from ever going to his Church again and stormed out of our house.

It is important to note that the Holy Spirit was my wife's teacher, and she received all her teaching directly from God. She read the Bible for hours in a day. The Holy Spirit taught her by reading from the Bible with him giving her the understanding of what she had been reading.

She also prayed to God and asked that she would only receive True Teaching from the Holy Spirit and not be deceived by others. This was a problem for many pastors of churches we went to. She stopped going to Church because they were trying to destroy her faith to justify their control over the congregation. They were not submitted to the Holy Spirit's leading and were not preaching the true Gospel of Jesus Christ.

Please understand that I am not against Churches or Pastors, and I am just reporting the facts of what happened when she became a Christian in Bunbury in Western Australia.

## Jesus' Vision for his Church

### John 13: 34

*A new commandment I give to you is that you love one another; as I have loved you, you also love one another. All will know that you are My disciples if you have a love for one another.*

# CHAPTER 9

## The Future of the Church

THE HOLY SPIRIT TELLS many Christians that we are entering a Golden Age of abundance and blessing. In a vision in 1995, when Jesus appeared to me and took me into heaven, he clearly stated the Church was entering a Golden Age, which would include the restoration of Apostolic Offices.

Everyone in the Church would have an office not just the Pastor. The Holy Spirit will be poured out on all flesh as it is written. I believe this age is called the *Age of the Holy Spirit*.

I believe this will have a major impact on the Church and the way the Church operates. Holiness is ownership. **We are Holy because Jesus owns us**. Because Jesus owns us, we are set apart for his purpose and glory. We cannot earn Holiness by obeying the Law.

The Church will change from being a keeper of the Law and ensuring Christians are keeping to the rules to a Church—where Christians are being transformed into the likeness of Jesus by the leading of the Holy Spirit. **Those whom the Spirit of God leads are Sons of God.**

In the new Church, worship will be a major focus; **true worship is obedience to God.** Christians in the New Church will obey God and the Holy Spirit.

Music worship will become the Church's main focus, and I believe some churches will have a room set apart for 24 hours of worship with a team of worshippers holding continuous worship 24/7. This will allow people to walk into churches on a 24-hour basis. Also, this will affect Satan's kingdom as he does much of his work at night.

The sun rules the day, and the moon rules the night.

That was why the Holy Spirit got me to pray between 1:00 and 5:00 am.

In speaking about revival, churches, and whole communities can have revival. It is very simple; all required is to obey the Holy Spirit and meet in one accord.

The Kingdom of God does have a structure. So, the new Church will have a structure as ordained by God (Not men).

We are called to go into all the world and preach the Gospel.

### *Matthew 28:17*

*Jesus came to them and said, "All authority has been given to me in heaven and the earth; go therefore and make disciples of all nations, baptizing them in the name of the Father and of the Son and the Holy Spirit."*

### *Mark 16:15*

*Go into all the world and preach the Gospel to every creature.*

### *Luke 46-47*

*Thus, Christ needed to suffer and rise from the dead on the third day; repentance and remission of sins should be preached in his name to all nations beginning at Jerusalem.*

Jesus wants us to focus on preaching the Gospel to the lost. We need to go out of our Churches into the community and preach the good news that God so loved the world that He gave His only Begotten Son that whoever believes in Him shall not perish. Moreover, for whoever believes that Jesus is the Son of God, Jesus gives them the right to be a Child of God and receive the Gift of Eternal Life. Jesus will never leave or forsake them, and they have received the right to eternal life.

The Holy Spirit will give us the power to preach the Gospel.

The Apostle Paul said, *"I did not come with wise and persuasive words but a demonstration of God's Power. Your faith may not rest on men's wisdom but God's Power"*.

God will confirm the Gospel message with signs and wonders following.

### Hebrews 2:4

*Is God also bearing witness with signs and **wonders**, various miracles, and gifts of the Holy Spirit, according to his own will?*

# CHAPTER 10

## The Circumcision Party

My purpose in writing this section is to understand that there is a circumcision party that opposes the Holy Spirit's leading. The purpose of the circumcision party is to take back the authority they lost when Jesus tore the temple's veil from top to bottom.

The circumcision party theology says it is not enough to believe in Jesus; you must obey the Law of Moses. The main work of the

Circumcision Party is to oppose the work of the Holy Spirit.

They judge people as being Christian or not by the person's theology or keeping the law of Moses. Alternatively, they say you have to have a degree in Theology. As I stated before, there is only one test of the spirits, any spirit or person that cannot say Jesus Christ is their Lord and Saviour is not from God.

You will find that many leaders in the Circumcision Party cannot say that Jesus is their Lord and Saviour, and even some bishops or heads of mainline denominations cannot say Jesus is their Lord and Saviour. To some, their position is just a career where they will get a healthy retirement package after many years.

I say these things through my own experience; some years ago, I was invited to a Men's breakfast to farewell a retiring bishop who was sick and unwell. I asked if I could pray for him, and he agreed. So, after everyone had left, I prayed for this man, but the Holy Spirit said, *"Ask him to say that Jesus is his Lord and Saviour."* He could not.

We prayed for him to give his life to Jesus and be filled with the Holy Spirit; he wept as he was filled with the Holy Spirit and confessed that it was the first time in his life that he had experienced the love of Jesus.

People have asked me many times about my theology.

The Holy Spirit is my Teacher, Guide, and Counsellor. He will tell me what to say, show me all things of Jesus, and bring me to full knowledge and understanding.

**The Holy Spirit is unlimited wisdom**; *why would I rely on my brain and intelligence when I can rely on the Holy Spirit?*

As it is written, *trust in the Lord with all your heart, lean not on your understanding, in all your ways acknowledge him, and he will direct your paths.* **Cursed is every man who trusts in man and not in God.**

All Christians and churches are part of the body of Christ; we all have different functions. Therefore, *a finger cannot judge a toe; the ear cannot judge a mouth.* **It is our master Jesus who judges us and makes plain all things that are hidden.**

This section suggests that those who move by the leading of the Holy Spirit will be persecuted by those who are not led by the Holy Spirit but operate using rules, regulations, and judgment.

I suggest some sections of the Church Denominations may be operating under the Temple System and the Law of Moses. I suggest this has been my experience in some instances.

This opposition from the Circumcision Party came the first time the Holy Spirit led Peter to go to the Gentiles.

Peter received a vision of unclean animals for eating, and then he was told to go with the men seeking him. God said that anything unclean was clean if he declared it clean. The result was that Peter went to the Gentiles to the house of Ananias, and the Holy Spirit was poured out on the household of Ananias.

### Acts 10:45

*Moreover, those of the circumcision who believed were astonished, as many as came with Peter, because the gift of the Holy Spirit had also been poured out on the Gentiles.*

Then the Circumcision Party complained about Peter going to the Gentiles.

### Acts 11: 1-4, 16-18

*Now the apostles and brethren in Judea heard that the Gentiles had also received the word of God. Moreover, when Peter came up to Jerusalem, those of the circumcision contended with him, saying, "You went into uncircumcised men and ate with them!".*

But Peter explained it to them in order from the beginning, then I remembered the word of the Lord, how he said, *"John indeed baptized with water, but you shall be baptized with the Holy Spirit."*

If, therefore, God gave them the same gift as He gave us when we believed in the Lord Jesus Christ, *who was I that I could withstand God?* When they heard these things, they became silent; and glorified God, saying, *"Then God has also granted the Gentiles repentance to life."*

The Circumcision Party waited for a more suitable time and continued with their doctrine and teaching that believing in Jesus Christ was not good enough. You still need to be circumcised and follow the Law of Moses.

### *Acts 15:1*

*Moreover, certain men came down from Judea and taught the brethren, "Unless you are circumcised according to the custom of Moses, you cannot be saved." The Circumcision Party continued its doctrine and caused great division in the early church.*

### *Galatians 2:1-17*

*When Peter had come to Antioch, I withstood him to his face because he was to be blamed; for before certain men came from James, he would eat with the Gentiles; but when they came, he withdrew and separated himself, fearing those who were of the circumcision. Moreover, the rest of the Jews played hypocrite with him, so even Barnabas was carried away by their hypocrisy.*

*However, when I saw that they were not straightforward about the gospel's truth. I said to Peter before them all, "If you, being a Jew, live in the manner of Gentiles and not as the Jews, why do you compel Gentiles to live as Jews? We who are Jews by nature, and not sinners of the Gentiles, knowing that a man is not justified by the works of the law but by faith in Jesus Christ, even we have believed in Christ Jesus, that we might be justified by faith in Christ and not by the works of the law; for by the works of the law no flesh shall be justified."*

# CHAPTER 11

# The Works of God - through me and others

I AM WRITING THIS section to encourage you that I am no one special, yet God has used me to do amazing things, sometimes instantaneous answers to prayer.

## (1) Drug-Induced Episode

A Pastor friend phoned me to say his granddaughter was having a drug-induced episode in a park in Perth, WA. She was shouting, screaming, abusing, and attacking people, and the police had been called. He was afraid she would be arrested. I said I would pray immediately. He phoned me back after some 5 minutes to say she was now in her right mind, very calm and peaceful, and they were taking her home before the police arrived.

## (2) Prayer Meeting at Christian Bookshop

I was invited to a Prayer Meeting by in a Christian Bookshop in Bunbury by Claire Conroy. Before the meeting, I was asked to go and pray for the Lady who owned the bookshop. It turned out that after she started the bookshop, her husband turned against her and left with all her finances, and her daughter also left. She was about to go bankrupt with no way to pay her debts.

After I had prayed for this lady, I drove back to Perth, on the way back in the car, (Some 15

Mins Later) the lady owner of the Book Shop phoned me, she just had a phone call from the man that owned the lease on the shop, he had heard about her problems, He cancelled all the debts she owed him for leasing the shop, he also gave her an additional 3 months of rent for free until she sorted out her problems.

## (1) Instant Cure of Stroke Victim

I went to work in Perth by Train starting at 6:00 am and returned to Midland Station at 6:00 pm. It was a long day.

When I got off the train at the station, there was an Aboriginal man with a stroke shuffling along with the platform. He could hardly walk. He was bent over, his legs were crossed, and just shuffled one foot at a time, and his arm was bent across his chest. The Holy Spirit said, *"Go and pray for that man."* I said, *"No, I have had a long day at work. I do not want to pray for that man."*

As I walked past the man, he looked at me and said, *"Sir, please can you help me?"* I said, *"What would you like me to do for you?"* He said, *"I do not know."* I said, *"Would you like me to pray for you to be healed?"* He said, *"Yes, please."*

I prayed for him, a very brief prayer and not very respectful.

I said, *"Be Healed in the Name of Jesus"* to my amazement, his legs uncrossed, he stood up straight, he became at least 4 inches taller, his arm became normal, and he just took off walking very quickly down the platform overtaking people. I had to apologize to the Holy Spirit and was taught not to limit God in any situation. I want to stress that my faith was not involved in this healing. However, what was involved was that I had favour with God.

## (2) Meetings

In 2003, I was sent to Bunbury to hold Home Group Meetings and raise warriors. Claire

Conroy and I held many Friday evening meetings in the Girl Guide Hall, the Bunbury Awakening Event at the Bracknell Shell, home group meetings, and meetings in other churches in Bunbury.

Many people were blessed by these meetings and prayed to be filled with the Holy Spirit. Claire's ongoing ministry to the homeless, alcoholics, and drug addicts, with other Christians, has helped the revival in Bunbury, which has started and is increasing in strength.

I am sure many people in Bunbury's Prayer and ministry contribute to this revival which is increasing in power even as I wrote this in 2020. However, many who were called were not faithful and gave up because of the opposition of Satan.

I understand it is difficult when we are in the middle of a war and want the persecution and the attacks to stop. People should expect attacks *(1 Cor 16:9)*. What I find strange is that most of these attacks come from people in churches whom Satan is using to try and stop this move of God.

The main strategies for advancing this revival are obedience to the Holy Spirit and spiritual warfare.

### *Eph 6: 10 & 2 Cor 10:3-6*

*We do not wrestle against flesh and blood, but principalities, against powers, against the rulers of the darkness of this age, against spiritual hosts of **wickedness** in the heavenly places. My prayers have been against the Prince of Bunbury and Satan's Kingdom in Bunbury and the Southwest.*

Since 2014, I have held many meetings in Western Australia or supported other ministries in Bunbury, Guildford, Bassendean, Thornlie,

Brookton, Merredin, and Kalgoorlie, and attended many prayer Bible study meetings. There have been hundreds of people touched by these meetings and ministries.

I have adopted Paul's mentoring model, where he prayed for Timothy to be filled with the Holy Spirit and receive spiritual gifts, and then Paul mentored and supported Timothy.

Therefore, I have always offered to support people and their ministry when I have prayed for them and laid hands on them to be filled with the Holy Spirit and Fire.

However, I am careful to tell them not to listen to what I say; they must check with the Holy Spirit.

I am not allowed to become more important to them than Jesus.

# (3) Aboriginal Ministry 2019

In January 2019, I held a meeting at Brookton, WA, which started a ministry to Aboriginals. I included the continuation of my other work to assist in the start of a revival.

The main people involved with the Brookton meetings were Laurie Johnson and Alan Little, where I met Pastor Murray Yarran and Gloria Watkins.

In January 2020, since Brookton, we had prayed with hundreds of people and saw the amazing transformation of lives, deliverance, healing, baptisms, and whole remote communities turning to God. Revival among Aboriginal People has started, and this ministry is now ongoing and increasing.

I believe revival has come to the Indigenous Peoples of Australia and will spread to Indigenous people globally.

Australia is the great southland of the Holy Spirit.

It is already starting to include Papua New Guinea, New Zealanders, and Philippines. I prayed with Gloria Watkins to be baptized in the Fire of the Holy Spirit, she was massively touched by God, and we started a relationship where I supported her ministry (Shalom Ministries) and others working with her including Martin, Kath, Elishia, Norm, Judy.

**The following are some of the things we experienced following the Brookton Meeting in January 1999:**

### Badjeling Easter Crusade: Easter 1999

Pastor Murray Yarran invited me to the Badjeling Easter Crusade (Badjeling is an aboriginal community about one and half hours outside Perth near Quairading.)

I was surprised when I got there on Friday, and Murray told me I was the Guest Speaker for the Crusade for the next 3x days.

So, on Friday, I gave two teachings/sessions.

1. *The spies who went to the Promised Land and became afraid of the Giants, how God was displeased with them*

2. *The Kingdom of God versus the Kingdom of Satan*

At the end of the second session, I prayed for several people to destroy the Giants in their lives.

In between, people were giving personal testimonies or singing or sharing. Norm was there and some others, singing songs, playing their guitar, and sharing.

Then Murray asked me to close that day in prayer.

# THE NEW HOLY SPIRIT AGE

I prayed that all God ever wanted was to have a relationship with people, believe what he said, obey his commands, and love him.

It was very cold. I stayed up all night sitting around the fire and praying, and everyone else went to bed. For me, it was a very special spiritual time with God, and I managed to do much praying.

The next day Saturday was relaxed until the afternoon.

Then there was a remembrance service for Murray's Mum, Myrtle Yarran.

Afterward, a very interesting thing happened. While I was walking back and forth across the field parallel to the stage and behind the people sitting around the fires. I became aware that on the left-hand side was a very holy tree where they used to hold Christian services under the tree.

On the right-hand side of the field was a tree where evil was dwelling. I could see a demon and some evil spirits.

I asked the Holy Spirit what I should do; he said to watch what happens. Next, I saw the Demon, and the spirits started to get very agitated. Miriam, an elder, went forward; she said God had shown her a vision of a Tank of Water close to the field. The tank had a pipe with a valve, the valve was open, and water was coming out and making the field wet.

She went forward to close the valve, but God said, *"No, do not close the valve; this is my blessing for the Badjaling Aboriginal people. This blessing is the Holy Spirit and the revival that will come forth upon the Badjaling People."*

She said that God had instructed her to invite the people to go forward, and she would pray for them to receive the Holy Spirit.

No one went forward. I felt led to go forward. I was the only person to go forward. Miriam told me she was very disappointed. She said God would give me whatever I asked for. I asked that I might receive the blessing and the Holy Spirit on behalf of the Badjaling People. She prayed for me, and I stood in the Gap and received the blessing on their behalf; the anointing was very strong.

The next day Sunday, Laurie Johnson arrived. I said to Murray that he should give out the easter eggs I had brought for the kids and then lay his hands on each one to receive a blessing and that the kids be filled with the Holy Spirit, so some of the Littlies and older children went forward, and Murray prayed for them.

Then Murray asked me to speak.

I told them they had been very stupid, like the spies sent out into the promised land and allowed the Giants to intimidate them. I also explained that when a prophet of God speaks and tells them what God says when they decide not to obey, they are not disobeying the Prophet but the God who sent the prophet.

I told them not to be concerned as I had received the blessing on their behalf.

I told them I wanted them to understand why they could not receive the blessing; there was a demon in the tree at the edge of the campsite, and this Demon had cursed them.

A Maori lady spoke and said she could confirm what I said; her phone had rung, and she walked over to the tree not to disrupt the meeting, and she saw the Demon and confirmed what I said; Laurie also confirmed there was Demon in the tree.

I said that the Elders of the Badjaling People should pray and remove the Demon after the meeting, then I asked all the people to come forward and receive their blessing. Everyone came forward, including teenagers and children, around 70 people.

They formed 3x rows; I invited others who felt led by the Holy Spirit to come and minister; the Maori Lady, Laurie, and Murray, and I ministered to the people.

It was very powerful with God delivering and blessing people and healing people; it went on for more than an hour, but I am not sure of the time. When it finished, this Lady came forward and said that God had told her they should pray against the Demon now while the whole people were assembled; Murray agreed, so the Lady prayed with backing from others.

There were some very gifted Aborigines, Maories, and Papuans; and Laurie who were able to see in the spirit and relay to the people what was happening as the Lady prayed, she prayed for the demons' weapons to be destroyed, and a bolt of lightning came from heaven and destroyed his spear, it went up in flames. She prayed he would run from his enemies, and he left the tree and started running, then she prayed he would be bound, and the gifted people saw a rope come down from heaven and wrap the Demon in strands of thick rope so you could not see his head or feet.

Then she prayed that God would take him to the place assigned for him; gifted people saw a whirlwind come down from heaven, lift the wrapped Demon, and take him off out of their sight.

It was an amazing experience, many people were awed, and God's fear came down on the meeting.

Murray then closed the service, and everyone agreed that the Crusade had been an amazing blessing.

I started to pack up my sound system, but it took over an hour as people kept coming up and asking me to pray for them, not just older people; quite a few teenagers asked me to pray for them. So, I believe the Crusade went very well and was a massive blessing to many people.

I also believe it was the start of the revival that the Badjaling people had been praying for.

## Aboriginal Communities

Gloria Watkins and her team were invited to Remote Aboriginal Communities in Kimberly. I went to pray and support the Shalom Ministries Team of people.

I believe that when the ministry team was in the remote communities, over 50 People gave their lives to Jesus, and many were prayed to be filled with the Holy Spirit. I went up onto the high places and prayed to bind all the Power of Satan in that place. The enemy suffered a massive defeat, and the door was opened to the full gospel message.

The team also prayed for the community from high places.

The Holy Spirit led Martin to place a cross on a High Hill overlooking the community, and with members of the Kimberley, it took two hours to walk up onto the hill. One young boy thought Jesus had come back when he saw the cross, and the people of Kimberly put another cross on the other side of the community led by an older man (Joey) who had the same word from the Holy Spirit as Martin.

The first meeting was held on Sunday when we got there.

The meeting was held at an Aboriginal Church of approximately 30 persons.

The meeting lasted 3 ½ hours; the Church was not in a building but just outdoors with a circle of chairs. Gloria prayed for the people one at a time; many were healed and filled with the Holy Spirit.

Some of those were Law Men who got delivered and received Jesus as their saver. Many young children and teenagers also prayed for healing, receiving Jesus, and being filled with the Holy Spirit. Some people were also baptized in the river.

I believe revival has started in aboriginal communities in Kimberly. I estimate that Gloria has prayed for approximately 3,000 people, an update on Gloria's ministry.

## (4) Obeying the Holy Spirit

Even though this happened some years ago, I felt led to include this to stress the importance of being led by the Holy Spirit.

An American Indian came to work in the office next to me; he was an atheist and hated God.

The Holy Spirit said, go to his office and say, *"The father's sins shall be visited on the Children even up to the Third Generation."*

He became very angry and asked me to leave his office.

*"Thanks, Holy Spirit, that did not go too well."* The next morning, he came to me and said, *"I am sorry I was so angry yesterday; I have been thinking about what you said. My father left my mother and me when I was very young; we had no money and lived in poverty; I hated my father for his actions. So, when you said I would receive my father's sins, I was very angry, but later that evening, I thought, how can I not receive my father's sins? Then it came to me, If I give my life to Jesus, all my sins will be forgiven, and I will not receive my father's sins."* So, I prayed for him to

*give his life to Jesus, for him to be filled with the Holy Spirit"*, and then he asked me to baptize him in my swimming pool.

Shortly afterward, he went back to America.

Some 5 years later, I met him at a friend's house in Capel near Bunbury. He told me that when he went back to America, he witnessed to 42 of his relatives, all American Indians, and prayed with them so they could give their lives to Jesus.

I was amazed that my obedience led to 42 people receiving Jesus and even more as the 42 themselves became witnesses.

About the same time, before the revival meeting in the Church.

I felt led to stand up in the Church of St. Nicholas Australind and say if you obey the Holy Spirit, there will be a great revival; people will walk off the streets and give their lives to Jesus.

At the end of the meeting, two ladies came up to me very excited; they said after you finished speaking did you see what happened.

I said no. they said after you finished speaking, a man walked into the Church, he was very confused, took him to a room at the back of the Church, prayed with him, and gave his life to Jesus.

God is seeking those who worship him in spirit and truth

**True Worship is obedience to the Holy Spirit.**

*See Chapter 16: Revival in Bunbury in 1999.*

# CHAPTER 12

## My Journey

MANY YEARS BEFORE MY birth, my mum was a Christian in the Welsh revival, and my dad intended to become a catholic priest. With the second world war, both appeared to have lost their faith in God.

It is hard to explain this; it is just my belief that when I was born, I believe I was born filled with the Holy Spirit from the Welsh Revival.

Within a day of my mum leaving the hospital after my birth, Satan tried to kill me. My mum and dad were sitting outside a pub at a table; I was left in the car park only some yards from where they were sitting, my mum felt led to go and pick me out of the car, and two minutes later a low loader truck carrying a huge excavator came round the corner, and the excavator shovel swung and fell onto the car and crushed the spot where I had been lying in a carrycot, if my mum had not gone and fetched me, I would be dead.

I was very advanced for my age; I think this was the Holy Spirit. When I was two years old, I read the newspaper to my dad while he was having his evening meal; most children could not read until they were 4 years old and went to school. When I was 4 years old, I told my mum and dad I wanted to attend church and Sunday school. They said I could go, but I would have to take myself there as they did not want me to go. So, when I was 4 years old, I walked some 20 mins to Church on Sunday on my own. Later at 7 years, I joined the Choir and went to Church thrice each Sunday; then, later, I became a server (helped the Priest with communion) and went to Church twice a Sunday; in my teenage years… I helped run the church youth club. This continued until I was 15 when my music teacher died, and I fell away from God.

A very interesting thing happened around thirteen while going to Confirmation Class; there were around 12 of us sitting around a small table; the Priest was talking about the Holy Spirit; suddenly, I felt like electricity, and all the teenagers started laughing, the Priest became very angry as he could not stop them laughing. He dismissed the class, and we all left still laughing.

Some years later, I realized this was the Holy Spirit, and similar things happened in other moves of God. (John Wimber Conferences)

So, I drew close to God for many years and then fell away; I was not very Holy and was very close to being an Atheist until 1990.

We had moved to Bunbury, and a Christian spoke to my wife and me and challenged me to read the Bible and believe in God. He said I would not understand the Bible unless I asked God for the understanding. So, I prayed a very irreverent prayer, *"O God, if there is one which I do not believe there is, please give me the understanding to read the Bible."*

So, I started one hour a night, then 2 hours, 3 hours, and eventually, I read the Bible for up to 5 hours a night. I understood what I was reading and had a hunger to know more about God. I read that God spoke to Abraham, Isaac, Jacob, and all the prophets; some did not seem very Holy, especially David, so I believed God would speak to me. So, I started to hear the voice of the Holy Spirit, it began as a very quiet voice, and I just learned to hear that voice until it became much clearer, and there was no doubt that the Holy Spirit was speaking to me.

At the same time, I started to spend two hours each morning with the Holy Spirit before I went to work; he would teach me and guide me and specifically tell me which scriptures he wanted me to read and then give me teaching from those scriptures.

Our first attempt at joining a church did not go well, and we were banned from the Church after 6 weeks. My wife's parents came to Australia, and we felt led to join a church for their sake. (We were asked to leave the first Church we went to.)

I remember when we joined this new Church, after the service, at morning tea, just in general conversation, I started to say the Holy Spirit told me this or the Holy Spirit taught me this, a lady came up to me and took me to one side, she told me the people in this Church were not filled with the Holy Spirit. They did not understand what I was telling them, as most of them were not filled with the Holy Spirit.

The Priest of that Anglican Church, Joe Hopkins was a very godly man and filled with the Holy Spirit, so under his guidance, I flourished in that Church; however, after he left, under the new Priest and his wife, I was extremely persecuted, she had a Jezebel Spirit and a hatred of men because she had been raped in earlier years.

She saw me as an extreme liability because of my prophetic gifting, which I heard from God. So, they concocted a complete lie story and had me thrown out of the Church.

Then the Priest went to the Bunbury Brothers Fraternal and continued lying about me until the pastors wrote a letter to every Church in Bunbury saying I was not from God.

My reason for writing the above section is to give wisdom and understanding that if the Spirit is leading you, there is a strong possibility you will be persecuted.

Even as I wrote this in February 2020, I left my current Church. I have been going there for 15 months, and for 15 months, I have been asking them to let me hold a Holy Spirit-led Meeting on a Friday night in the Church Hall.

They have finally admitted they have no intention of letting me hold a meeting. (I have been holding meetings outside the Church in Public Halls on a Friday evening or weekend in Western Australia for many years)

I have been given many wonderful works to do by God in the last 20 years, and I want to encourage you that I am not anyone special and you can carry out healings and miracles as the Holy Spirit directs you.

I think it would be useful if I explained how the Holy Spirit leads me. It is sometimes difficult to hear the Holy Spirit.

Thus, I pray, *"In the name of Jesus I bind my mind, in the name of Jesus I bind Satan, in the Name of Jesus I only want to hear from the Holy Spirit."* Then I believe whatever I heard is from the Holy Spirit, and I acted on it.

I will then have a further confirmation where I feel the presence of God like a heavyweight, and then I feel the heat across my shoulders and neck or stomach. Then sometimes, I shake gently, and then I feel my heart rate increase dramatically as the time for me to act or speak passes.

When the Holy Spirit speaks to me, I always ask three questions

1. *Do You want me to pray about this?*

2. *Do you want me to do something?*

3. *When do you want me to do this?*

Sometimes you have to have patience when God asks you to do something and keep asking the Holy Spirit—*is it now? Is it now? Etc.*

I often wait to speak to someone until the Holy Spirit says *"no"* even when I run out of patience, *God will have his way.*

I was in a church in Darwin about 6 weeks ago. I asked if they wanted revival and if I could speak in their Church—they declined. After Church, the Holy Spirit pointed out a man to me in the kitchen area and said I want you to pray for that man. I waited and waited, and in the end. I lost patience and walked out of the Church to the car park. I heard someone running behind me so I turned and saw this man. He said, *"I was watching you in the ser-*

*vice, and I have not seen anyone who appeared so spiritual in our Church and wanted to speak to you."* I replied, *"Would you like me to pray for you to be filled with the Holy Spirit?"* He said, *"Yes, please."* So, in the car park at the side of the Church, I prayed for the man. As I prophesied over him, he started crying. As he composed himself, he told me that what I said was exactly what he prayed that morning when he asked God to bless him.

Therefore, I repeat that every one of you can do mighty things for God. **You need to be led by the Holy Spirit and spend time with God.** Spending time with God will give you favor, and Jesus will call you a friend.

I spend two hours most nights speaking to God, praying, and carrying out spiritual warfare over various subjects and countries and all sorts of different things.

Some of my prayers are instantly answered. Some are taking longer. I prayed for America, Trump, the Impeachment, the UK, Boris Johnson, Brexit, and Israel. I pray for nearly every nation globally and locally for Australia.

When we foster that special relationship with Jesus and the Holy Spirit, God will make us Co-rulers and show us what He wants to accomplish in the world.

# CHAPTER 13

## Baptism

As an introduction to this Baptism section, God sent me to an Anglican Church some years ago. The Holy Spirit led the Priest of this Church, Joe Hopkins, and I came to admire this man as a true man of God.

As part of the healing team of this Anglican church, I went to VMTC Meeting/Training (Victorious Ministries thru Christ)

(This is a Prayer Counselling System that tries to be led by the Holy Spirit)

The VMTC Organisation in WA was made up of Churches that professed to be Pentecostal and some Anglican Churches. The Holy Spirit powerfully led some ministers, but they were a minority. The Pentecostal Pastors and Anglican Priests started arguing about infant baptism. I was unaware of this argument, and the Holy Spirit woke me at around midnight and gave me teaching on Baptism, which I wrote down. It supported Infant Baptism.

In the morning, I told the people running VMTC that the Holy Spirit had given me this Teaching on Baptism and could I share it—they said no, so I sat down. Later in the day, I shared with Joe the Teaching I had been given about Baptism; he became angry and said I should have stood and given the teaching even when the Leaders said I could not.

I said no, I have to obey the Holy Spirit, and he would not lead me to speak in rebellion.

To summarize, God will briefly support in his court of law in heaven any promises or contracts undertaken by God's Parents or others on behalf of children.

The Holy Spirit explained that this was similar to me standing surety for a loan at a bank.

If my son wanted a loan but did not have enough of a deposit or ability to repay the loan, then I could stand surety for the loan, and based on my promise and signing as guarantor, the bank would give him the loan.

Therefore, any pastor teaching that baptized infants in a church will go to hell is false.

I need to say that I was baptized as an infant, but later I was led by the Holy Spirit as an adult to be baptized by full immersion in the sea. Therefore, I am not proposing any specific theology except to say that **the Holy Spirit must lead us in all matters.**

Theology is not as important as being led by the Spirit of God.

Interestingly, just two weeks before writing this, the Priest, as part of the sermon in the Church, asked for a show of hands as to who had been baptized as a child, who had been baptized as an adult, who had been baptized by full immersion. I was surprised that I was the only person in the congregation who raised my hand to all three questions.

I am not saying I am any better than anyone else. I just found it interesting.

# CHAPTER 14

# REVIVAL STARTS IN AUSTRALIND, 1999 (BUNBURY REVIVAL)

REVIVAL START 1999 – St Nicholas Church, Australind, Bunbury Western Australia.

This is the email I sent following the Revival on Sunday.

From: Mike Shenton on 08/11/99 07:53

To: linden.roper@alcoa.com.au, ahandley@southwest.com.au, nick.mehanikov@alcoa.com.au

cc:

Subject: Revival has started

Hi guys

On sunday the priest Glen started his sermon and then suddenly stopped and asked the question what is the purpose of a prophet, he got a number of answers, but said the job of a prophet was to listen to the word of god and to tell the people what god was saying.
He said in todays church as soon as a prophet speaks what god is saying the church turns on the prophet and throws him out, the church is not willing to listen to god or take the time to find out what he is saying.
Therefore he said let us have some time in silence to listen to what god is saying and if someone believes god is saying something to the church they should come up the front and speak.
After a while a young lad of around 17 came up to the microphone, and as he stood there about to speak the anointing came down on him, this big grin came over his face, and whenever he tried to speak he could not, he looked exactly as if he was drunk, but without falling around, he just stood there almost in a kind of stupor.
As he stood there one guy stood up and said this man is not drunk as you suppose, but this is what the rophet Joel said that in the last days god would pour his spirit out on all flesh, another guy stood up and said he had a vision of a door, it was just slightly ajar, but god wanted that door fully open, after what seemed a long time the young lad was eventually led back to his seat and sat down, he had difficulty walking on his own.
Glen then invited others to come up and speak, only one got up and read a passage of scripture, I cannot remember what it was for by this time the anointing was very heavy on me and I was listening to the holy spirit, he told me to go to the microphone and speak,
When I started speaking I heard myself say that 2000 years ago the disciples knew how much god loved them because jesus walked amongst them, they were able to look into jesus' eyes and see the love, they were able to hear his voice and to hear the love, they were able to feel jesus' touch and to feel the love, but he told them I am

*Mike Shenton*
*Design Engineer*

# THE NEW HOLY SPIRIT AGE

going to the father but I will send you another comforter, the holy spirit, he will teach you he will guide you, he will comfort you he will reveal the love of jesus to you. It is the job of the holy spirit to make jesus real, you cannot know jesus or his love unless the holy spirit reveals jesus to you. Therefore please come forward so that we can pray for you and ask the holy spirit to reveal the love of jesus in your life. Glen the priest also encouraged people to come forward and about 20 came to the front of the church, I then invited all those who felt led by the holy spirit to come forward and pray for those already out the front, and about another 20 people came to pray for those already at the front.

I started praying for this lady and I started to feel this great wave of love coming, I said I could feel this love descending over her and she said she could feel it as well, the next thing she burst out crying and thanking god for how muched he loved her, this crying spread right through the people standing at the front, and also out into the congregation where dotted here and there were other people crying, and others in the congregation gathered around and prayed for them. I had never seen anything like this in any Anglican church before. I went and sat down and left the others to minister, this went on for quite some time ,

eventually Glen gave the call to share the peace, but those upon whom the holy spirit had fallen carried on weeping, and those who were ministering carried on ministering, so some people were going round shaking hands and sharing the peace while others were praying and ministering.

Eventually Glen started the offertory song, and the people went and sat down although many of them were still weeping,

Then we went into communion with still a few people weeping, then we came to the end of the service, the guy who had the vision of the door got up and spoke, and declared that the door was now fully open, but also he had a vision that the church had been dragging around this ball and chain which was bondage, and that this ball and chain had been completely smashed into powder this very morning, however he warned that the church must not move back into bondage but must move forward as the holy spirit leads them.

After the service some of the people gathered into groups and were praying for each other.

I went into the vestry room to pray and thank jesus for the wonderful thing he had done, the next thing Glen comes in with a few other ladies and we start praying for him, the holy spirit came upon him quite powerfully, and more people came into the tiny room which eventually became crowded, and they were alll praying for each other

*Mike Shenton*
*Design Engineer*

and laying hands on each other, I slowly worked my way round to the door and left I felt led to leave them to minister to each other.
Although it was quite some time after the service had finished the car park outside was still full of cars, normally when I leave there is only 2 or 3 cars in the carpark.
So it was a really glorious service, I was just amazed by what the holy spirit did that morning and I know it can only get better.

Isn't this exciting news. I will keep you posted on further developments.
Regards
Michael Shenton

It Is interesting that in 1999, a Revival Started in Bunbury, Western Australia. Before the revival, I went to the Church every day for some months and worshiped for an hour.

I was a worship team member, so I could switch on the sound equipment and worship using the keyboard.

The presence of God and the anointing of the Holy Spirit got stronger.

After the revival, I could not go to any of the churches in Bunbury and speak in those churches.

Bunbury had a very strong Brothers Fraternal (Group of Pastors and Priests).

Before this revival, they had already had meetings to complain about me, decided I was not from God, and issued letters to the Churches not to have anything to do with me.

They soon managed to squash/crush this revival. They did not want to lose control. I asked them if they wanted revival in their Churches. *"Could I come and speak in your churches?"*

They said that this revival had nothing to do with me as I was not from God, and I was deceived, probably from the Devil. They wrote a letter to every Church in Bunbury saying I was not from God.

Stuart Devenish, who was Chairman, did not agree with the rest of the Pastors, but he was overruled. I have great respect for Stuart Devenish, a true man of God. So, a 20-year period followed where I was not allowed to speak in the churches in Bunbury, and I received hostility and persecution from most of the Pastors.

This persecution continued even when I went to meetings in Perth. This persecution continued even when I went to the John Wimber Conference in Perth. The Pastor of the Perth Church organizing the John Wimber conference repeated what was said in Bunbury that I was not from God. I said, *"But what is the Holy Spirit saying about me?"* He replied that he would prefer to listen to the Pastors in Bunbury rather than the Holy Spirit.

The exciting news is that this season has finished, and this revival that started in 1999 is now breaking out again in Bunbury and getting stronger and stronger. In 2022 the revival is getting much stronger and will see a massive outpouring of the Holy Spirit in many parts of the world.

In 2014, I was taken up into heaven and had a meeting with Jesus to discuss the Revival in Bunbury; this included meeting with the council of Elders for the Gentiles. (There are two councils of 12 Elders - 12 for the Tribe of Israel and 12 for the Gentiles)

They discussed the coming revival, and I listened. I was told who the main players would be. I was surprised that it took so long as I had the feeling the revival was imminent. Still, I should not have been surprised as some of the things the Prophets spoke took over 2000 years to come to pass.

The revival that started in Bunbury is progressing and growing stronger and stronger. It is good to see many Inter-Church Prayer Meetings taking place. I have some other evidence regarding the start of the Revival in Bunbury, which I feel is useful to share. In 2013, I was sent to Bunbury to raise warriors and start a home group, the size of the home group varied from 8 to 20, and when I left Bunbury in 2016, I continued to hold a Friday Evening Meeting in Mary Street Girl Guide Hall in Bunbury.

There would be 20–30 people at these meetings from different churches.

In 2014, after a home group meeting, a demon came into my bedroom and sat on my bed. He looked very strong, powerful, and heavy, and my bed went down where he sat.

I asked the Holy Spirit what was happening. He said this is the Prince of Bunbury; he has come to intimidate and frighten you so that you will stop your work. I commanded the demon to get off my bed and leave my room, and he left thru the wall.

# THE NEW HOLY SPIRIT AGE

In 2016, the same demon appeared in my room again; he looked very thin and not very powerful and was more respectful. I asked the Holy Spirit why this demon had come, and the Holy Spirit said He had brought the demon to show what effect my prayers had on his kingdom in Bunbury and the South West. Most nights, between 2:00 am, and 4:00 am, I would get up and pray for whatever the Holy Spirit wanted me to pray for.

In 2018, the demon appeared in my bedroom again. This time I could see through the demon, and he kept fading in and out; I got the impression that he almost did not have enough power to sustain himself in our dimension. The Holy Spirit said I want to show you the effects of your prayers and others. He has completely lost control of Bunbury and the South West, and the revival in Bunbury is getting stronger and stronger so that its fullness will manifest very soon.

# CHAPTER 15

## The New Apostolic Age

I wrote this book in 2003, but I cannot take credit for writing this book. All the comments/summaries below refer to the book *"The New Apostolic Age."*

This book is written like a manual. I know many who use this book as a *"How do I do this"* type of book.

On Friday, while at work, the Holy Spirit told me I want you to start writing a book this evening.

I started writing the book on my laptop at approximately 5:00 pm Friday, I was given the Title and the Chapters first, and I just typed as instructed by the Holy Spirit.

I typed from Friday evening to 7:00 pm Sunday (I do not remember the time exactly). I took some time off to sleep, so I typed the book in two and a half days.

When I read the book, I did not agree with some things, and the Holy Spirit declined when I wanted to change those things. This was a blessing for me as Pastors often tried to have a Theological discussion/argument with me about this book. I could say I did not write the book, so you need to take up your problem with the Holy Spirit.

I have assembled the summary of the book into a series of messages:

## Message 1: The Vision

In 1995, while in my office at work, I was visited by Jesus and transported into the heavenly realm. His main message was that the Golden Age of the Church was about to start, and this would be ushered in by the restoration of the Apostolic Offices of the Church. He said the Pastors and Priests were not allowing the other church offices to minister. He said he was restoring the ministry to lay people.

There would no longer be an elite priesthood controlling everything.

## Message 2: spend time with God. (The most important message in this book.)

Even on a work day, I would get up early and spend at least 2 hours in God's presence, where the Holy Spirit would teach me or show me things from the Bible. Alternatively, I would pray for someone or a circumstance. Alternatively, I would be instructed to go and do something. Sometimes this 2-hour used to go very quickly on earth but a long time in the spirit.

At this point, spending time with God has increased dramatically.

## Message 3: God will speak to you.

I read in the Bible that God spoke to Abraham, Isaac, Jacob, the Prophets, The Apostles, etc. So, I believed God would speak to me if He spoke to all those people.

In my case, God spoke to me with a small quiet voice in my mind. I had to learn the difference between God's Voice and my voice. One useful hint is that God speaks first, and your voice or Satan has to speak second.

When the Holy Spirit speaks to us, Satan will immediately try to say that it is just your voice and we do not have to obey or listen to that voice or what it says. All sorts of logic will be proposed as to why the first voice is wrong and should not be obeyed.

One of the prayers I used and still use is this: *I bind my mind in the name of Jesus, I bind Satan in the name of Jesus, Holy Spirit, I only want to hear from you, in Jesus' name, amen.*

Then by Faith, I would obey or say what I was instructed to say or do. There is no condemnation for those in Christ Jesus. There are no mistakes, only opportunities to learn more. Do not be concerned if things do not go as you expect. A father always loves his child regardless of anything that appears to be a mistake. If God is in control of the whole universe, I am not sure if he can make a mistake.

# Message 4: Unconditional Love keeps no record of wrongs

One of the most important messages of Jesus was on forgiveness—He said if you are at the Altar with a gift and have unforgiveness against someone, go and forgive that person so your gift will be accepted. A father always loves his child regardless of the mistakes they make. I know that forgiveness is the cause of many sicknesses and diseases in our bodies. Someone once said unforgiveness is like drinking poison and expecting others to die.

**We must hate the sin but love the person.** If we have a problem with someone, we can love them but bind the spirit operating thru them. I have heard Christians say that they hate Satan. I do not think this is correct; even the angel of the Lord was respectful to Satan. I have met Satan in person. The angel that introduced me to Satan was respectful to Satan. However, he was direct with his words and told Satan very clearly that I had been given all authority—authority and power over Satan and his kingdom thru the name of Jesus.

*There is Faith, Hope, and Love,* **but love is the greatest of these three.**

## Message 5: Spiritual Warfare

Our warfare is not against flesh and blood but against the principalities and powers of the air. One gifting may be intercession and Spiritual Warfare. One of my commissions is to raise Warriors to conduct Intercession and Spiritual Warfare.

Many years ago, I was taken to heaven and met with Jesus and the council of 12 Elders for the Gentiles. (24 Elders—Revelation: 12 Elders for the Tribes of Israel and 12 Elders for the Gentiles) They discussed the coming Revival and how I needed to raise Prayer Warriors.

I spend a lot of time in prayer / spiritual warfare—at least 2 hours a day, including fasting. I have fasted 40 days twice and regularly fast for 3 days every couple of days. I suggest you will have a greater victory if God leads you too fast.

If the Holy Spirit asks you to fast, you will have greater success.

I am FIFO at a mine site and sometimes have to stay overnight at a hotel. I pray from 10:00 pm until 7:00 am. My flight is three and a half hours, so I also spend time praying while on the plane.

I pray for many countries and governments and situations globally and locally.

Whichever city I find myself in, I go and pray in that city against the local powers of Satan, and the prince over that region, the strongmen in that city, the gatekeepers of the roads, waterways, and airways. I have people phone me and ask me to pray for a situation to be fixed, and the result is normally instantaneous. I am now finding that God uses me in a situation even when I am asleep.

For examples of where God uses me, refer to the NHSA—Recent Works section.

## Message 6: Being born again

Whoever believes that Jesus is the Son of God will be given the right to become children of God.

(that is—Born of God—Born again by the Holy Spirit)

> Jesus said, *"Surely I say to you, unless one is born again, you cannot enter the Kingdom of God."*

That which is born of the flesh is flesh, that which is born of spirit is spirit, do not marvel that I say to you must be born again. This is different from receiving the Holy Spirit or being filled/ baptized with the Holy Spirit. In Acts, it says that they had been baptized in the name of Jesus and had not received the Holy Spirit.

Therefore, people must receive the Holy Spirit thru the laying of hands by people who have this power and are authorized to give the Holy Spirit.

## Message 7: Being filled with the Fire of the Holy Spirit

John the Baptist said, *"After I come one whose sandals I am not worthy of losing, he will baptize you with the Holy Spirit and Fire."* The Baptism of the Holy Spirit and Fire differs from being born again.

> Jesus said, *"For John truly baptized with water, but you shall be baptized with the Holy Spirit not many days from now."* Moreover, again, Jesus said, *"You shall receive power when the Holy Spirit has come upon you."*

Baptism of Fire is life-changing; the first disciples were given the power to evangelize the world using signs and wonders after the Baptism of Fire.

Peter and John went to them and laid hands on them so that they might receive the Holy Spirit. It was seen that the Holy Spirit was given by the laying on of the Apostle's hands so much that Simon the Sorcerer offered them money so he could have this power that anyone on whom he laid hands would receive Holy Spirit.

## Message 8: The Keys to Apostolic Anointing

The keys to Apostolic Anointing are mainly written in the lives of Jesus' Disciples as they grew spiritually into Apostles.

1. *Belief in God*

2. *Belief in Jesus*

3. *Jesus is the Father, is the Son, is the Holy Spirit; they are separate and one*

4. *Meeting the Jesus of Nazareth*

5. *Meeting the Risen Jesus*

6. *Meeting the Glorified Jesus*

You only need the above to receive Apostolic Anointing God decides who receives this anointing. Still, we are encouraged to pray for and ask for this ministry and all spiritual gifts, for God will grant your heart's desires if your motive is pure and unselfish.

Another blessing that you can receive at higher levels or lower levels as God determines.

7. *Meeting the Father*

8. *Meeting the Holy Spirits*

9. *The Ministry and Spirit of Elijah and Moses*

10. *Your Personal Key—given to you by the Holy Spirit*

*How do you know your level?* **Close your eyes and start praying to God.** *Who do you see that is your level?*

## Message 9: Gifts of the Holy Spirit

The gifts of the Holy Spirit are available to everyone.

You must realize that they are gifts, and Jesus gives them to whomever He wants. The power which operates with the gift is directly linked to your relationship with Jesus.

It is not linked to your goodness or lack of sinful nature.

You cannot earn the gifts. The main gifts are as follows:

1. *Prophecy*
2. *Revelation*
3. *Visions*
4. *Speaking in tongues*
5. *Praying in the spirit*
6. *Traveling in the spirit*
7. *Translation*
8. *Transfiguration into Glory*
9. *Healings and Miracles*
10. *Deliverance*

There are, of course, fruits of the spirit: ***Love, Joy, Peace, Patience, Goodness, Kindness, and Self-control.***

## Message 10: The Works

When we are fellowshipping with God, listening to the Holy Spirit, and willing to step out of our comfort zone and obey the leading of the Holy Spirit, then God will give us works to do.

These works will start small and grow as we become better at listening to the Holy Spirit and become more obedient to the Holy Spirit. The Bible clearly says that God has prepared works for us to do.

The Power of God operating through us depends on our relationship with God, the Lord Jesus, and the Holy Spirit.

Because of my time in God's presence, the Holy Spirit sent me to do many things.

One of the most amazing was when Revival came to St. Nicholas Church in Australind in Bunbury.

## Message 11: Persecution

If you hear from God (if God has chosen you for a specific task in his kingdom work) and if the Holy Spirit gives you instructions and you obey them, you will be persecuted. (This persecution will generally come from the Church and not the world.)

Satan will attack you to stop the damage you are executing on his kingdom. Satan will counterattack whenever you have a victory.

## Message 12: Restoring the Offices of the Church, Apostle, Prophet, Evangelist, Pastor-Teacher

God's plan for the church is as Paul said in Ephesians:

*It is he who gave some to be apostles, some to be prophets, some to be evangelists, some to be pastors and teachers, to prepare God's people for works of service so that the body of Christ may be built up until we all reach unity in the Faith and the knowledge of the Son of God and become mature, attaining to the whole measure of the fullness of Christ.*

However, some church leaders do not want us to come to the full measure of Christ; they suggest we cannot have a relationship with Jesus unless we go thru them.

Human organizations have appointed them; sometimes, many do not believe in Jesus. To them, being a priest or a pastor is just a career or a job leading to superannuation and retirement.

They persecute those people that have been appointed by God and are operating under the direction of the Holy Spirit. They give great Theological Sermons, but the Holy Spirit does not lead their teachings.

The Apostle spoke of this when he said:

> *I did not come with wise and persuasive words but a demonstration of God's power so that your faith may not rest on man's wisdom but on God's Power.*

In the beginning, Moses was the Prophet and God's Representative. Moses was spoken to by God and instructed the people to carry out God's Commands. Aaron was the Priest and was there to serve Moses and carry out his instructions.

God said that Moses was to be like a God to Aaron.

Later the Priests of the Temple took control; they persecuted or killed any prophet of God who was a threat to their authority.

The Temple Priesthood persecuted and destroyed Jesus because He was a threat to their human structure of authority, whereas Jesus' authority came from His Father.

This system is still operating today. In Galatians, Paul clearly warned about the Circumcision Party, which was the re-establishment of being under the law of Moses and nullified the Crucifixion and Power of the Lord Jesus Christ. Paul called this a *false Gospel*. Anyone who operated according to the Holy Spirit was accused and destroyed by the Circumcision Party.

Under this system, it is not good enough that Jesus died and paid the price for our sins. You still have to obey the law to be justified or accepted by the Church hierarchy.

Even Peter was attacked by the Circumcision Party when he first went to the Gentiles.

## Message 13: The Desert Experience—being Tested

Christians today do not seem to be taught that one of the reasons they are here is so that God can test them. Unless you have gone through a desert experience and have been tested like Jesus was tested by Satan, you will never emerge with real power and authority in your ministry for God. And Satan will always have a hold over you.

We need to be patient, resist Satan, and he will flee. The battleground is in mind. If you have the Word of God inside you, it will be easier to defeat Satan and pass the Test.

## Message 14: The Blessing

If you obey the Holy Spirit, you will be blessed.

**If you continually disobey the Holy Spirit, you will be corrected—even unto death.**

The blessing you receive is spiritual, but as the spiritual and the physical world are very closely linked, you will also experience blessings in health, wealth, relationships, etc.

Those that the Spirit of God leads are sons of God.

Therefore, we must obey the Holy Spirit to receive blessings.

## Message 15: Being Full of the Holy Spirit

> Jesus said, *"Anyone who has faith in me will do the works I have been doing. He will do even greater things than these because I go to my Father. I will do whatever you ask in my name so that the Son may bring glory to the Father. You may ask me for anything in my name, and I will do it."* He said, *"If you love me, you will obey what I command."*

> Moreover, again Jesus said, *"If you remain in me and my words remain in you, ask whatever you will."* He goes on to say, *"If you obey my commands, you will remain in my love."*

It is God's will for us to be full of the Holy Spirit and receive Apostolic Anointing, but it depends on our obedience to the leading of the Holy Spirit.

## Final Message 16: Revival

I used to live in Swansea, just a few miles from where I lived. God used Evan Roberts to start the Welsh Revival in Loughor in 1902-1904.

Wales was transformed into a Godly Country, and the effects lasted nearly 70 years. Even when I was a Teenager in the 1970's you could see the effects of the Revival.

Pubs were not allowed to be open on a Sunday; slowly, this rule was overturned. Morning assembly in schools was a Christian meeting; slowly, around 1970, this was attacked and later overturned so that Christian assembly was no longer held in school.

If you build your Faith, spend time with God, have a heart for God and His Kingdom work, and obey the Holy Spirit, your city, town, or church will have Revival.

In 1999, God used me to bring Revival to St Nicholas Church Australind; God has used me to bring personal Revival to many people who then went on to do great things for God.

When I have prayed for people to be filled with the Holy Spirit, I have supported their ministry and helped them be on fire for God. This is the model Paul used with Timothy.

# CONCLUSION

I WANTED TO ADVISE that I am available to go to any Church and speak or pray for people to be filled with the Holy Spirit. I have made a video series of each chapter of this book and placed the videos on YouTube.

The most important teachings are:
Your Right to be a Child of God
and Impartation
and the Laying of Hands

(This includes me praying for people Unconditional Love keeps no record of wrongs Satan has no weapons against unconditional Love.)

# ABOUT THE AUTHOR

Michael Shenton was brought up in Swansea, UK, in a council house estate. He originally joined the Welsh Church of England when he was 4 years old until he was approximately 14 years old.

Michael was in the Church Choir and a Server at Church Communion / Evensong for 4 years. He moved to Bunbury, WA, in 1987 and later became a member of the Anglican Church Healing Ministry Team run by Joe Hopkins.

While in the ministry, Michael saw many healings and minor miracles during that time.

In 1999, God called Michael to start a Revival at St. Nicholas Church Australind, WA. He received his Prophetic Office from Paul Cain and his Apostolic Office from John Wimber.

Michael's ministry is like Paul's to Timothy. He prays for people to receive the gifts of the Holy Spirit and then prays for their ministry to be in God's providence continually. He also trains and mentors the members and supports them in their ministry's needs.

Michael is not and has never been interested in the gains of his ministry but is rather more interested in supporting and uplifting others.

Michael's ministry is very simple—he listens to the Holy Spirit and carries out whatever the Holy Spirit enlightens him to do.

Personally, Michael had met Jesus several times, not in a vision but face-to-face. Also, he had been to Heaven approximately over 30 times. This meeting with Jesus and being taken to Heaven is available to anyone, same with John and Paul, who met Jesus and were taken to Heaven, and Michael does not see that he is any different from them.

Despite the rare opportunity of witnessing and feeling God, Michael still sees himself as no one special. He thinks anyone can do what he does if they have unwavering faith in God and a formidable relationship with Him.

Michael hopes that his experiences with God encourage you to never be afraid in seeking and creating your spiritual journey with Him.

www.ingramcontent.com/pod-product-compliance
Lightning Source LLC
Chambersburg PA
CBHW061758070526
44586CB00023B/2619